Time is precious. The clock ticks, obligations loom, chores call, and children r
that we can all give. Our time translated into the gift of a card says volumes
little piece of myself, my love, my time." What a gift! **The wonder that is created by a handmade card says something that even the most celebrated poet cannot.**

There have been many times in my life, when someone has done something that touched me in a special way. It may have been just a smile. It's often been a gesture of kindness or a simple act of service. It's been manifest through the good neighbor who responds to my situation with "Hey, let me help you out with that!" It's the co-workers who help me even if it isn't their job, or the sincere receptiveness of a listening friend. Sometimes it's been my sons or daughter who have done a chore without being asked. It's the teacher whom I realize loves my child too, or the doctor who shows me true compassion and empathy. There are also times when I just want to give, simply because I love someone and want to let them know.

It just takes a moment to give a gift of the heart. In my family we call it a positive ripple — like the ripples that expand outward when a stone is thrown into a calm pond or lake. I can't count the times I've had a skip in my step because of someone's thoughtfulness. It is one of the wonders of this life, those tiny gifts in the moments that make up each day, those gifts that bring us sustenance and peace. It's that **quiet wisp of grace - the gap between where we are now and where we want to be.** It's a moment that makes us feel like we want to be our best selves. It creates in us a desire to give back, not out of obligation, but because it feels good and flows from our heart.

When I find myself savoring a friend's sweet act of kindness, I often think, "I should do something really nice to let them know how much I appreciate them and how their kindness has affected me or my family." Unfortunately, most of the time I get caught up in my hectic schedule. I forget those marvelous gifts that I've been given. My best intentions go unfulfilled and become a tiny strand of memory that too often is lost. The gift becomes a fleeting smile that fades because its cause or effect was not celebrated.

From this day forward, let us celebrate these moments! Let's give ourselves license to seize each precious minute. Feel, express and share each sorrow, hope, gratitude and joy! Play hooky from the "musts" and "shoulds" of our busy lives, and truly take the time to recognize the magnificent wonder and blessing of the people and things that are our gifts. It has been said "to give is to receive." How true this can be — for all of us.

Desirée Tanner

Sizzix™ shapes shown have been altered and do not reflect actual die sizes. Sizzix™ Dies used: Grass, Circle #1 (ladybug), Fun Serif Uppercase "B" (butterfly), Oval #1 –Trimmed (bee body), Confetti (snail eyes), Swirl (on snail's shell)

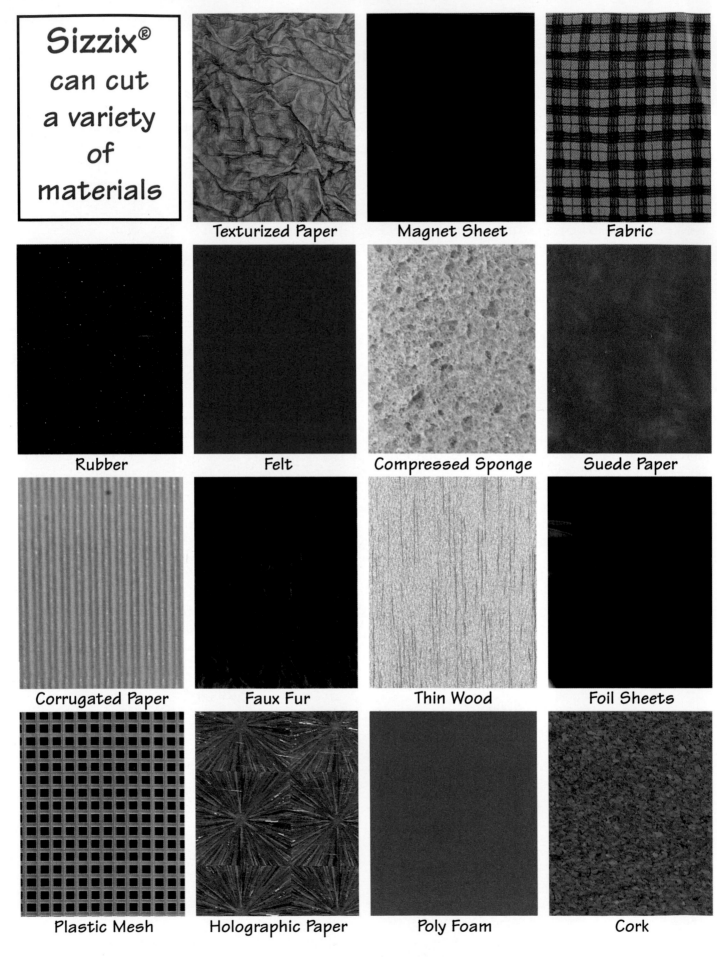

**Sizzix®
can cut
a variety
of
materials**

Texturized Paper

Magnet Sheet

Fabric

Rubber

Felt

Compressed Sponge

Suede Paper

Corrugated Paper

Faux Fur

Thin Wood

Foil Sheets

Plastic Mesh

Holographic Paper

Poly Foam

Cork

all of these and more...

GETTING READY

The first step is to become organized. Not a complete overhaul mind you, no spring cleaning involved - just a few tips and helpful hints. **Organization is an attitude, as well as an action.**

The Attitude:

First we all need to get past those roadblocks that block creativity and hinder organization. These are those voices that whisper, "You don't have time," or "You're not creative." Let's deal with those right now. No one just <u>has</u> time. We set aside time for the things that are important to us. We carve out niches in our daily routines to feed the pleasure of giving and loving. We reward ourselves for getting a chore done with allowing ourselves to bask in our creative glow. Think about what is important to you and set aside time to do it. Enjoy it, revel in it . . . This is *your* time!

It's not about being creative, it's about BEING! Celebrating moments of love, appreciation, beauty or even silence can be so satisfying! Sometimes stopping to listen to the hum of the earth, the breeze, or even our own breath can awaken that powerful creativity that flows from all of us. Translating this into a gift that comes from our souls through our hands is truly a gift of the heart. There is nothing more precious than that!

The Action:

We all need to devote a few moments to clearing off and cleaning up. It is so refreshing to walk into my office each morning to a bright shiny desk just waiting for me to create something on, or be productive at. In contrast, it can feel futile and feed anxiety to have to come into a messy space with the need to complete a task. It is worth the extra time to ritualize the cleaning process. Try to think of it as your last task of the day, something you do just for you, to give a little gift to yourself in the morning.

Here are a few tried and true tips that have helped me take all of my creative clutter and transform it into my own little creative paradise where magnificent gifts are able to be born. **Labeling:** I have storage containers that are labeled with each crafty item that I possess. This took me quite a few hours to organize and label, but it's brought me many days of clarity from my previous clutter. I love going to the "Ribbon Bits" drawer and knowing that snippets of my favorite ribbons will greet me. Or opening up my "Eyelets" drawer and finding the hole punches and setting tools right there with my eyelets. Label each drawer with a square cut from the Sizzix® Squares die-cut with a sample of the drawer's contents glued to it! **Separating:** There are handy drawer organizers that you place into existing drawers. These separate each item and section off drawers so that all of your scissors are together, and all of your adhesives are in one space. I have a container for my writing supplies, scrapbooking supplies, card making supplies and gift wrapping supplies. When I want to create something, I just pull out the appropriate drawers or containers, and I have everything I need! I used to spend frustrating hours searching for all of the supplies that I needed for a project. Now, I spend more time creating and less time ferreting out needed items. **The Right Tools:** The right tools can make any job a breeze. (Knowing how to use them correctly also helps.) Here are a few tools that I use over and over again. They save time and get the job done: **1.** Sizzix Machine (If I could have only one crafting tool, this would be the one. Now I can quickly cut any shape myself, out of tons of materials, as often as I need, for any purpose, in the convenience of my own home!); **2.** Sizzix® Dies (save hours of tracing and cutting); **3.** The Sizzix® Die Storage System (a must for organizing your dies). This storage system comes on a Lazy Susan base that turns easily and allows you to have virtually all of your dies at your fingertips; **4.** Xyron Machine (Xyron machines are handy roller machines that apply adhesive, laminate and magnet backing to any paper surface); **5.** Glue Dots (These little guys stick stuff together that nothing else will); **6.** Terrifically Tacky Tape Sheets (If you ever want to apply glitter or beads to a shape, these sheets are a must-have and Sizzix cuts them beautifully); **7.** Glue Pen by Zig. I like this one and it doesn't have a tendency to dry up quickly; **8.** A good pair of Scissors with a sharp point; **9.** Lots of Cardstock and Lighter Weight Patterned Paper (I love the Little Sizzles Paper Pads that fit perfectly under a large die – no trimming necessary!).

Getting Down To Business:

I've included a supply list at the beginning of every project. This will help you to gather what you need quickly. It may also be helpful to use it as a shopping list the next time you're at your favorite craft store. Each project has a clock next to it, indicating an approximate construction time for each project. There are also a few technique **Tips** to help you along and make each card just a little easier. Hopefully, they'll also inspire you to explore the wonder of your own creativity and encourage you to create your own little miracles in the form of gift cards. Some of these techniques are helpful to read even before you begin any of the projects. Alternative sayings are listed that can be substituted on the front or inside to express a different meaning. This allows you to make several of the same card, yet personalize each one with the meaning that meets your needs. Be sure and jot down your own ideas for titles or sentiments on each page!

Let's make some cards!

Chapter One

CUTTING CARDS ON THE FOLD

CUTTING CARDS ON THE FOLD

Cutting on the fold is a quick and easy way to make a folded card or shape in one easy step.

To cut on the fold, simply fold a sheet of paper in half. The size of the paper sheet you choose will depend on the size of the die you're using. Place this folded sheet underneath your die, being careful to place the folded edge just inside the right side of the die shape. Place the die rubber side down on the cutting pad, slide under the press, pull the handle, and you've got yourself a folded card that opens from the left hand side!

Each of these folded shapes has several uses. They work beautifully for cards of course, but they also do double duty in your scrapbooks. It's fun to tuck small photos, private messages or journaling into the folds of shapes or cards on the pages of your treasured memory albums.

There are several variations to cutting on the fold:

Cutting on the fold allows you to choose the orientation of your card. You can cut on the fold to have your card open from the top, bottom, left or even the right hand side. The typical orientation of opening cards is from the left, but it's ok to create a custom card that meets your own needs.

Here are some easy rules for cutting on folds other than the left hand side:

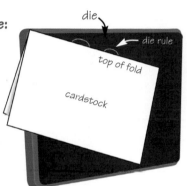

Fold on the Top: Position the fold just *under the top* of the die shape.

Fold on the Bottom: Position the fold just *above the bottom* of the die shape.

Fold on the Right Hand Side: Position the fold just *inside the left hand side* of the die shape.

Accordion Folds:

To make an accordion style fold, just fold your paper or cardstock back and forth, making sure that neither fold touches the cutting blade on either side of the die shape. Both sides should fall just inside the outline of the die shape. It's also important to realize that the Sizzix® Machine isn't designed to cut more than three sheets at a time. The Sizzix machine is designed to cut up to three sheets of paper at a time. That equates to a paper accordion folded twice. For longer borders, tape smaller segments together.

Creating the Inside & Outside of the Card at the same time:

It's always pleasing and cohesive to see a theme repeated from the front of a card to the inside of a card. One way to do this easily is to combine two coordinating printed papers and adhere them, back to back with a Glue pen or Xyron machine. This allows you to fold this sheet (now with a different coordinating front and back), and die-cut it on the fold, creating a card that repeats a coordinated theme or color as you open it. When using milled cardstock that is the same color on the back as it is on the front, you won't need to use this method.

Now that you know the basics, you're ready to go!

Remember, **it's not about being creative, it's about BEING!**

Chapter
Two

QUICK CARDS AND TAGS

Quick Cards And Tags

One of the most joyous and rewarding feelings in the world is to give freely. I love picking out just the right color of paper to go with a bouquet of fresh flowers, or tying the perfect tag onto a gift. It is wonderful being able to express my feelings or wit in a way that only the recipient will understand or find humorous.

It doesn't take long, and it doesn't have to be a masterpiece. Just a simple thought expressed or a note that says "I appreciate you" can be all it takes to brighten someone's day.

Welcome Little One
Card

SUPPLY LIST: Sizzix® Die Small Block **Paper** Little Sizzles™ Paper Pad "Pastels" by Sizzix™ **Miscellaneous** Clear Alphabitties™ "Wedge White" by Provo Craft®, Carefree Collectible "Rattle" by Provo Craft®, Eyelet Setting Tool, Hammer by Simple Ideas, Thin White Ribbon, Scissors, Xyron Adhesive

Tip: Cut Block on the fold, on the right side of the design. Attach the eyelet to the front half of the card, allowing the recipient to attach the little rattle charm and still open the card to see the message inside. Trim around the front edge of the Block in pink cardstock for a finished look.

Actual Size: 2" wide x 1-7/8" high

Moon & Star
Tag

SUPPLY LIST: Sizzix® Dies Large Squares, Small Moon, Medium Primitive Star **Paper** Little Sizzles™ Paper Pad "Country" and "Classics" by Sizzix™ **Miscellaneous** Gold Eyelet by Doodlebug, Eyelet Setting Tool, Hammer by Simple Ideas, Gold Embroidery Floss, Scissors, Sewing Machine, Clear Nylon Thread, Xyron Adhesive

Tip: Tear the gold paper and adhere it onto the blue cardstock BEFORE die-cutting with the Moon die. Sewing on cardstock with a sewing machine or hand stitching gives a wonderfully professional look to any project!

Actual Size:
CARD 2" x 2"
MOON 1-1/4" wide x 2" high

7

THANKS & YOU'RE WONDERFUL
TAG

SUPPLY LIST: Sizzix® Dies Large Tags **Paper** Color Wheel™ Scrap Pad "Flamingo Pink" and "Ocean Blue" by Provo Craft® **Miscellaneous** Clear Alphabitties™ "Parlor White" and "Wedge White" by Provo Craft®, Ribbon (preferably with wire), Scissors

Tip: To make any of these "bitty quick tags" just tie both sides of the tag together with the wired ribbon and write a message on the inside OR outside. It's a great way to give the gift of a thoughtful word in about a minute!

Actual Size:
1-3/4" wide x
3-3/4" high

Actual Size:
1-3/4" wide x
3-3/4" high

DAISY
TAG

SUPPLY LIST: Sizzix® Dies Large Tags, Large Plant Pots, Small Daisy #1 **Paper** Bitty Gone Big™ "When the Wind Blows", "Summer Rays" and "Lost in the Woods" by Provo Craft®, Little Sizzles™ Paper Pad "Earth Tones" by Sizzix™, Cardstock **Miscellaneous** Raffia, Star Bradletz™

Tip: Highlight card by outlining everything with a black pen.

WATERMELON
CARD

CARD WITH MOUSE

SUPPLY LIST: Sizzix® Dies Large Circles, Bitty Pajamas & Bear (mouse) **Paper** Color Wheel™ Scrap Pad "Flamingo Pink" and "Ocean Blue" by Provo Craft®, Pink Cardstock **Miscellaneous** Alphabitties™ "Wedge White" by Provo Craft®, Teardrop Punch, Black Micron Pen by Sakura

CARD WITH BUTTONS

SUPPLY LIST: Sizzix® Die Large Circles **Paper** Color Wheel™ "Red" and "Spring Green" by Provo Craft® **Miscellaneous** Alphabitties™ "Parlor Black" by Provo Craft®, 3 Black Buttons, Twine

Tip: Use a black or white pen to add contrast to your cards by drawing a small line around the inner or outer edge. **Tip:** Use the two largest circles in the circle set to make the watermelon.

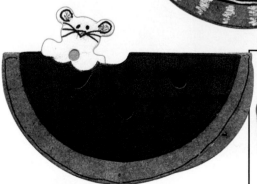

Actual Size:
2-1/4" wide x 1-1/4" high (without mouse)

8

BUTTON SUNFLOWER
CARD

SUPPLY LIST: Sizzix® Dies Large Daisy #2, Small Leaf #2 **Paper** Little Sizzles™ Paper Pad "Classics" and "Earth Tones" by Sizzix™ **Miscellaneous** Clear Alphabitties™ "Wedge Black" by Provo Craft®; Small Black, Dark Brown and Light Brown Buttons by Dress It Up; Art Accentz™ "Black Micro Beedz™" by Provo Craft®; Art Accentz™ "Terrifically Tacky Tape™" by Provo Craft®

Tip: To get a super crinkled look to your cardstock, get it totally wet, crinkle and let it dry overnight. Chalking it while it is still drying will increase the absorption of the chalk for a more dramatic effect. **Tip:** Cut the center portion of the Daisy out of your Terrifically Tacky Tape™ sheet. After trimming out circle and peeling off coating, press buttons onto Tape Sheet on center of Daisy. Now press Daisy center into a container filled with Black Micro Beedz™ to fill in the holes. **Tip:** You can also use the circles from the Circles die to make the center of your flower. **Tip:** Try using beads only to fill the center of any flower for a sophisticated look. **Tip:** Trim the petals to look like a sunflower.

Actual Size:
4" wide x 3" high

Hi Sunshine!

BLUE GINGHAM FLOWER
CARD

SUPPLY LIST: Sizzix® Dies Large Daisy #2, Medium Branch & Leaves, Small Swirl **Paper** Little Sizzles™ Paper Pad "Country" by Sizzix™ **Miscellaneous** Navy Heart Bradletz™ by Provo Craft®, White Gel Pen, Glue Pen by Zig

Tip: Place Bradletz™ on the flower center before adhering the center to the flower so that you can't see it from the inside of the card.

Actual Size:
3 1/4" wide x 3-1/4" high

LARGE BUTTON SUNFLOWER
CARD & ENVELOPE

SUPPLY LIST: Sizzix® Dies Large Daisy #2 (use the smaller Daisy on the die) Medium Branch & Leaves **Paper** Gold Cardstock, Little Sizzles™ Paper Pad "Earth Tones" by Sizzix™ **Miscellaneous** Clear Alphabitties™ "Wedge Black" by Provo Craft®; Coluzzle® Envelope Template, Guarded® Swivel Knife and Cutting Mat by Provo Craft®; Thin Green Twine, Scissors, Glue Dots, Xyron Adhesive

Tip: Try adding one large button instead of lots of little ones. Loop twine through holes in the button and tie a bow.

Hey Sunshine

Actual Size:
CARD 2-1/4" x 2-1/4"
ENVELOPE 2-5/16" x 2-5/16"

FOR YOU DAFFODIL
TAG

SUPPLY LIST: Sizzix® Die Large Tags **Paper** Little Sizzles™ Paper Pad "Pastels" by Sizzix™, Bitty Gone Big™ "Thyme and Again" by Provo Craft® **Miscellaneous** Vellum Stickers "Friends & Flowers" by Provo Craft®, Twine, Scissors, Black Micron Pen .03 by Sakura, Xyron Adhesive, Glue Dots

Tip: To make the vellum sticker really stand out, place it onto white cardstock and trim around it. For a more subtle look, place it directly onto the Tag. Thread the twine around the back of the flower pot and tie a tiny hand written note on a slip of white cardstock. Try making place cards with this same idea and writing each guest's name on the tiny tag.

Alternative Sayings:
"Thanks"
"If Friends were Flowers, I'd Pick You"
"Love Makes Everything Grow"

Actual Size:
3" wide x 2-1/2" high

TAG YOU'RE IT
TAG

SUPPLY LIST: Sizzix® Die Large Tags **Paper** Pathways™ "Illumination" Paper Pad by Provo Craft®, Little Sizzles™ Paper Pad "Classics" and "Pastels" by Sizzix™ **Miscellaneous** Pathways™ Clear Alphabitties™ "Traditional Black" by Provo Craft®; Coluzzle® Companion Circle Template, Circle Template, Cutting Mat and Guarded® Swivel Knife by Provo Craft®; Black and Silver Ribbon; Xyron Adhesive

Tip: Remember to adhere your paper back to back before you fold and cut with the die. This insures that the inside of your card is as beautiful as the outside! If you've been playing phone tag with a pal or associate, this is a sure fire way to get them to try a little harder to reach you. Including your number will get the message across!

THANKS
TAG

SUPPLY LIST: Sizzix® Dies Large Squares, Large Circles, Medium Leaf, Stem, Small Swirl **Paper** Little Sizzles™ Paper Pad "Watercolors" by Sizzix™ **Miscellaneous** Clear Alphabitties™ "Parlor White" by Provo Craft®, Scissors, Black Micron Pen .03 by Sakura, Xyron Adhesive

Tip: Use the two smallest circles from the Circles die to create your flower. Adhere the Swirl in the center Circle. Be sure and fold your flower patterned paper twice so that the inside of your card is patterned. Line around the outside of the front of the card to coordinate with your lettering inside.

Alternative Use:
This would also make an easy and versatile place card.

Actual Size:
1-3/4" wide x 3-3/4" high

Actual Size:
2" wide x 4" high

Actual Size:
1-3/4" wide x 3-3/4" high

PEACE
TAG

SUPPLY LIST: Sizzix® Die Large Tags **Paper** Little Sizzles™ Paper Pad "Earth Tones" and "Rainbow" by Sizzix™ **Miscellaneous** Bundlez™ by Provo Craft®, Wired Raffia, Red Buttons, Black Micron Pen .03 by Sakura, Xyron Adhesive, Liquid Adhesive by Tombow

Tip: Form a thin line of glue around your die-cut, and form your wired raffia along that line. You can add dimension to just about any die-cut using this method!

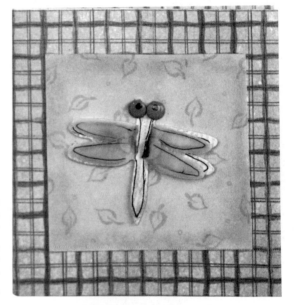

DRAGONFLY
TAG

SUPPLY LIST: Sizzix® Die Large Squares, Small Dragonfly **Paper** Little Sizzles™ Paper Pad "Pastels" by Sizzix™, Bitty Cone Big™ "In A Tree Top" and "Lilac Basket" by Provo Craft®, Vellum **Miscellaneous** Lavender Bradletz™, Black Micron Pen .05 by Sakura, Glue Dots, Xyron Adhesive

Actual Size:
3" wide x 3-1/8" high

THREE HEARTS
TAG

SUPPLY LIST: Sizzix® Die Large Tags **Paper** Pathways™ "Illuminations" Paper Pad by Provo Craft®, Vellum **Miscellaneous** Heart Shaped Eyelets, Hammer and Eyelet Setter by Simple Ideas, Pink Ribbon, Scissors, Xyron Adhesive

Tip: Cut the vellum Tag, then trim the sides down so that it's a little smaller than the Tag. Secure the vellum down with the heart shaped eyelets. Accordion fold paper twice and die-cut. Attach extra folded sections with adhesive.

Actual Size:
1-3/4" wide x 3-7/8" high

Chapter
Three

INVITATIONS &
COORDINATING
THANK YOU NOTES

INVITATIONS & COORDINATING THANK YOU NOTES

After our twin boy's sixth birthday "Puppy Party," my husband and I sat on the front porch steps; relieved, joyful, exhausted and a little sick from eating hot dogs and lapping up punch from our doggy bowls. The games ("Pin the Tail on the Doggy," "Doggy Obedience School" and every barking, rolling over, and fetching contest you can imagine) were all finished. Only a few stray balloons, a half eaten puppy shaped cake and a big mess remained. After the clean up, we realized that the only tangible things we had left from all of that fun were the photos and the "Puppy" themed invitation! We were so grateful that we'd taken a few moments to make an event truly memorable with a handmade invitation, that created joy in our lives and in those whom we love.

Actual Size:
5" wide x 4" high
OPEN 7-1/2"

WESTERN PARTY
INVITATION

SUPPLY LIST: Sizzix® Dies Large Circles, Medium Cowboy Hat **Paper** Brown SuedePaper™ by Wintech, Little Sizzles™ Paper Pad "Country" and "Watercolors" by Sizzix™ **Miscellaneous** Wired Raffia, Bundlez™ by Provo Craft®, Chalk by Craf-T Products, Clear or White Tiny Rubber Bands, Jute Woven Border, Black Micron Pen .03 by Sakura, Glue Dots, Glue Pen by Zig

Tip: To secure the bandanna onto card: attach only the front of back bandanna to back of the last hanging circle. Do not glue back of the front of bandanna to the bottom of the card. This way you can tuck the girl's chin into the bandanna to seal the card! Use glue dots to secure wired raffia hair underneath the SuedePaper™ hat.

WESTERN COWBOY BOOT
THANK YOU NOTE

SUPPLY LIST: Sizzix® Die Large Cowboy Boot **Paper** Brown SuedePaper™ by Wintech, Little Sizzles™ Paper Pad "Earth Tones" and "Watercolors" by Sizzix™ **Miscellaneous** Brown Suede Fringe, Black Micron Pen .05 by Sakura, Xyron Adhesive

Tip: Cut Boot on the fold using brown cardstock. Next, cut one Boot out of brown SuedePaper™. Adhere suede Boot on top of folded Boot. Tuck fringe underneath black cardstock trim on bottom of the Boot. Seal the fringe on top underneath black cardstock loop at top of Boot.

Actual Size:
3-3/4" wide x 3-3/4" high

LET'S BBQ!
INVITATION & COORDINATING THANK YOU NOTE

SUPPLY LIST: Sizzix® Dies Medium Hot Dog, Medium Baby Bottle **Paper** Little Sizzles™ Paper Pad "Earth Tones" by Sizzix™, Color Wheel™ Bitty Scrap Pad "Sunflower Yellow" by Provo Craft®, Bitty Gone Big™ "Little Red" by Provo Craft®, Vellum **Miscellaneous** Clear Alphabitties™ "Wedge Red" by Provo Craft®, Paper Shapers "Mini Scallop" by Provo Craft®, Scissors, Black Micron Pen .03 by Sakura, Xyron Adhesive

Tip: This could easily be used for an invitation for a Picnic, Birthday Party, or a creative invitation for a date to a baseball game. Just line the bun, dog and mustard and you'll be done with this quick invitation in less than 5 minutes! Use the Baby Bottle for the ketchup and mustard bottles. Just trim the top of the bottle to look like spouts. Make little labels, and you've expressed your thanks with relish! Tuck the completed hot dog into a vellum "wrapper" and send!

Alternative Saying:
"You're the Top Dog!"

For an Invitation Reply:
"We'll come, with Relish!"
"Thanks for coming. You brought the relish to our BBQ!"
"I'll Take You Out to the Ball Game-Will You Go?"

Actual Size:
INVITATION
3-3/4" wide x 2-1/2" high

Actual Size:
THANK YOU
2-7/8" wide x 3-3/4" high

Actual Size:
INVITATION
5" wide x
5-1/2" high

THANK YOU
1-1/8" wide x
1-3/4" high

YOU'RE INVITED TO A POOL PARTY
INVITATION & COORDINATING THANK YOU NOTE

SUPPLY LIST: Sizzix® Dies Large Doll Body, Large Doll Girl Hair #1, Large Doll Boy Hair #1, Large Squares, Medium Doll Summer Accessories, Medium Doll Summer Clothes, Medium Sand or Snow Mound, Medium Pool **Paper** Little Sizzles™ Paper Pad "Earth Tones", "Watercolors", "Country", "Rainbow", and "Pastels" by Sizzix™ **Miscellaneous** Chalk by Craf-T Products, Thin White Ribbon by Offray, Scissors, Black Micron Pen .02 & .05 by Sakura, Xyron Adhesive

Tip: To make the girl's arms stretch like this, just die-cut an extra Body and fold it down the center vertically. Cut the arms, extending all the way to the centerline (fold) of the body. Adhere these behind the girl's hair. Now use the feet of the extra doll to attach to her armpits, with the toes facing toward the center of her body. Secure the tops of the legs behind her hair. **Tip:** Trim the top of the Sand Mound to show more of the Pool.

Alternative Sayings:
"Bon Voyage"
"Come & Play"

SAILBOAT
INVITATION & COORDINATING THANK YOU NOTE

SUPPLY LIST: Sizzix® Die Large Sailboat **Paper** Bitty Scrap Pad "Ivory Coast" and "And Summer Too" by Provo Craft® **Miscellaneous** Canvas, Eyelets, Eyelet Setting Tool, Hammer by Simple Ideas, Red and Blue Star Buttons, Twine, Scissors, Gold Zig Pen .05, Red Micron Pen .05 by Sakura, Liquid Adhesive by Tombow, Xyron Adhesive

Tip: Xyron two pieces of Ivory Coast cardstock back to back. Fold. With the cutting side of die toward you, place fold just before the rule on right side of sailboat. This way it will open on the right side. Glue on top of Ivory Coast layer. Use the same instructions for coordinating thank you note, or just cut them out of a heavy cardstock to save time. Have your child help hand write what you loved about their gift or presence at the party.

Alternative Sayings:
"Bon Voyage"
"You are the Wind in my Sail"
"As you sail through your day, just remember that I love you"

It's been a pleasure

a Birthday Party for

set sail on an adventure

Actual Size:
INVITATION and THANK YOU
3-3/4" wide x 3-7/8" high

Actual Size:
THANK YOU
1-3/8" wide x
1-3/4" high

BEAR IN THE CARRIAGE
INVITATION

SUPPLY LIST: Sizzix® Dies Large Baby Carriage, Small Teddy Bear **Paper** Little Sizzles™ Paper Pad "Pastels" and "Watercolors" by Sizzix™, Bitty™ Scrap Pad "French Country" by Provo Craft®, Pathways™ Scrap Pad "Americana" by Provo Craft® **Miscellaneous** Clear Alphabitties™ "Parlor Sherbet" by Provo Craft®, Tiny Blue Buttons by Dress It Up, Flower Eyelets by Doodlebug, Eyelet Setting Tool, Hammer by Simple Ideas, Scissors, Black Micron Pen .03 by Sakura, Xyron Adhesive, Glue Dots

Tip: Use blue striped paper for base of the Carriage. Layer other cardstocks and patterned papers on top of base layer. Adhere Teddy Bear to back of the front of card. Use Glue Dots to secure buttons.

Alternative Uses:
This could easily be used for a baby announcement. By changing the color combinations, you could announce either gender – OR put two little Teddy Bears in the Carriage to announce twins!

p.s. boy

baby shower

baby shower

Actual Size:
INVITATION
4" wide x 4-1/8" high

PLEASE COME
INVITATION & COORDINATING THANK YOU NOTE

SUPPLY LIST: Sizzix® Dies Large Doll Body, Large Doll Girl Hair #1, Large Doll Overalls, Large Diamond #2, Medium Doll Summer Clothes, Small Bitty Swimsuit **Paper** Little Sizzles™ Paper Pad "Rainbow" and "Earth Tones" by Sizzix™, Flesh Cardstock **Miscellaneous** Clear Alphabitties™ "Wedge White" by Provo Craft®, Chalk by Craf-T Products, Paper Shaper Scissors "Mini Scallop" by Provo Craft®, Wire Cutting Tool, Heavy Gauge Wire by Artistic Wire, Wire Pliers, Green Raffia, Scissors, Black Micron Pen. 03 by Sakura, Xyron Adhesive

Tip: Decorate front Doll Body. Cut another Doll Body on fold at the top of head and attach to back of decorated doll for stability. Attach wire between the two layers of kite. Wrap wire around girl's hand. Tie with small pieces of raffia. Trim bottom of sandals with Mini Scallop Paper Shapers. **Tip:** To make these shorts, just trim the legs off the Overalls.

Alternative Saying:
"Let's Go Fly A Kite!"
You can also use this as a spring place card.

Actual Size: (without wire)
INVITATION GIRL 2-5/8" wide x 3-1/2" high
INVITATION and THANK YOU KITE 2" wide x 2-1/4" high

P-A-R-T-Y
INVITATION & COORDINATING THANK YOU NOTE

SUPPLY LIST: Sizzix® Dies Small Bitty Body, Small Bitty Boy Hair #1, Small Bitty Girl Hair #1, Small Bitty Dresses, Small Bitty Shorts & Top, Small Bitty Swimsuit **Paper** Bitty Scrap Pad "Tropical Colors" by Provo Craft® **Miscellaneous** Scissors, Black Micron Pen .03 by Sakura, Xyron Adhesive

Tip: Accordion fold paper twice and die-cut. Attach the hands of the last two dolls to the first three dolls with adhesive tape.

Actual Size:
THANK YOU
3" x 3"

Actual Size:
INVITATION
6-1/2" wide x 2" high

PLEASE COME
INVITATION & COORDINATING THANK YOU NOTE

SUPPLY LIST: Sizzix® Die Medium Candles **Paper** Bitty Gone Big™ "Summer Days", "Speckled Frog" and "Pink Lady" by Provo Craft®, Bitty™ Scrap Pad "Tropical Colors" by Provo Craft® **Miscellaneous** Alphabitties™ "Wedge White" by Provo Craft®, Ribbon, Black Micron Pen by Sakura, Sewing Machine

Tip: After cutting out the two Tags (one pink, one green) cut a square out of the middle of the Tag, then sew around the edge of the square with white thread.

Actual Size:
INVITATION 2-3/4" wide x 4-1/2" high

Actual Size:
THANK YOU
3/4" wide x 3-1/8" high

Actual Size:
THANK YOU
2-5/8" wide x
3-5/8" high

BALLOON PARTY
INVITATION & COORDINATING THANK YOU NOTE

SUPPLY LIST: Sizzix® Die Medium Balloons #1 **Paper** Purple, Green, and Pink Cardstock, Little Sizzles™ Paper Pad "Pastels" by Sizzix™ **Miscellaneous** 1/8" Circle Punch, Triangle & Rectangle Punches, Purple Twine, Black Micron Pen .02 by Sakura, Xyron Adhesive

Tip: Use entire sheet of white cardstock from Little Sizzles™ Pastels Paper Pad for front of card. Mat with green, then purple. Tuck ends of twine under cardstock at bottom of card.

Alternative Sayings:
To convert this into a Birthday Card, just write, "Happy Birth Day _____", putting each word under the four balloons.

Actual Size: INVITATION 5-1/2" wide x 7-1/4" high

LUAU
INVITATION & COORDINATING THANK YOU NOTE

SUPPLY LIST: Sizzix® Dies Large Palm Tree, Large Circles **Paper** Little Sizzles™ Paper Pad "Earth Tones" by Sizzix™, White Cardstock **Miscellaneous** Paper Party Umbrella, Chalk by Craf-T Products, Scissors, Black Micron Pen .03 by Sakura, Xyron Adhesive

Tip: Cut Palm Tree on fold at top out of white cardstock. Decorate with layers of patterned papers and cardstock. Draw little "hairy" lines out of the coconuts and put three little "holes" on each of them. To make Coconut Thank You Note, cut one Circle on the fold at top and decorate with layers behind and in front of the Circle on the fold.

Alternative Sayings:
"You're Invited to a Beach Party"
"Welcome Home from Hawaii!"
"We're moving to California!"

Actual Size:
INVITATION
3-1/2"wide x
5" high

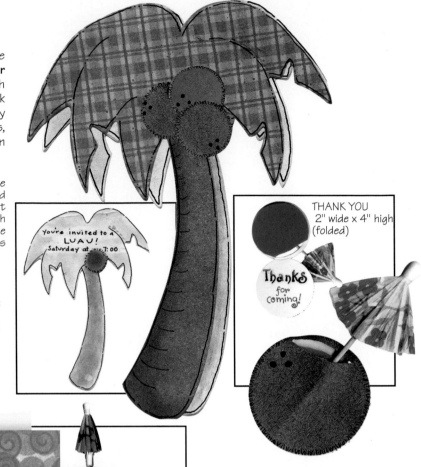

THANK YOU
2" wide x 4" high
(folded)

You're invited to a LUAU! Saturday at ... 7:00

Thanks for coming!

Actual Size:
THANK YOU
3-1/4" wide x
4-3/4" high
(folded)

We had the best time! love, the Tanners

PALM TREE WITH SAND
INVITATION & COORDINATING THANK YOU NOTE

SUPPLY LIST: Sizzix® Dies Large Palm Tree, Small Campfire (for plants) **Paper** Little Sizzles™ Paper Pad "Earth Tones" by Sizzix™, Bitty Scrap Pad "Bahama Blue" by Provo Craft® **Miscellaneous** Bradletz™ "Funky Flower" by Provo Craft®, Art Accentz™ "Terrifically Tacky Tape™ Sheets" by Provo Craft®, Fibers by Scrappin' Essentials, Sand by Sandtastic, White Paint Pen by Deco Color, Black Micron Pen .08 by Sakura, Glue Pen by Zig

Tip: Use glue pen to attach fibers to the trunk of the Palm Tree. **Tip:** Hand cut pieces of Terrifically Tacky Sheets™ to attach to the bottom of card. Dip into sand. Layer more pieces here and there at the bottom of the card to add a realistic look. **Tip:** Use the fire portion of the Campfire die to make flowing leaves or seaweed. **Tip:** Try wrapping Christmas lights or tinsel for a tropical Christmas Card.

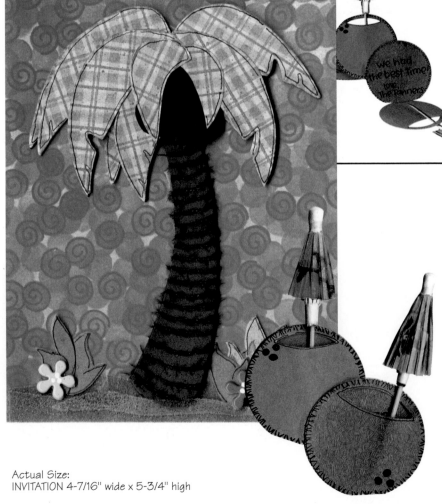

Actual Size:
INVITATION 4-7/16" wide x 5-3/4" high

PARTY
INVITATION

SUPPLY LIST: Sizzix® Dies Large Circles; Fun Serif Alphabet and Punctuation "P", "A", "R", "T", "Y" and "!" **Paper** Scrap Pad "Let's Party" by Provo Craft®, Little Sizzles™ Paper Pad "Pastels" by Sizzix™, Color Wheel™ Cardstock "Sunflower Yellow" and "Apple Red" by Provo Craft® **Miscellaneous** Font: "PC Wacky" This n' That PC HugWare™ CD by Provo Craft®, Red Curling Ribbon, Black Micron Pen .03 by Sakura, Xyron Adhesive

Tip: Cut a piece of red cardstock 8-1/2" x 7". Fold the cardstock in half so that the final dimensions are 4-1/4" x 7". Die-cut the letters and place on card. Layer patterned paper strips above letters. Type or write invitation information inside the card. Tuck the ends of the curling ribbon under the paper strips at the top of the card. Follow the same basic instructions for the coordinating "Thank You" card.

Actual Size:
INVITATION and THANK YOU 7" wide x 4-1/4" high

Actual Size:
THANK YOU 3" x 3"

TICKLED PINK
INVITATION & COORDINATING THANK YOU NOTE

SUPPLY LIST: Sizzix® Dies Large Tags, Large Daisy #2 **Paper** Bitty Scrap Pad "Flamingo Pink" by Provo Craft®, Little Sizzles™ Paper Pad "Country" by Sizzix™ **Miscellaneous** Alphabitties™ "Scrapbook" Fun-Multi Repositionable by Provo Craft®, Scissors, Cloth Covered Wire or Ribbon, Glue Pen by Sailor, Xyron Adhesive

Tip: Xyron pink and green patterned paper back to back. Fold back and forth twice just between the rule lines on large Tag die. Attach extra folded sections with adhesive. (This will allow you to accordion fold the invitation when it's done, and not cut off either side.) Cut Daisy on the fold, but cut another Daisy to lie on top of Daisy on the fold, so that each of your petals go all the way to the end.

Alternative Use:
This is also a great invitation for a garden party or any party in the spring or summer time.

Actual Size:
INVITATION 6-7/8" wide x 3-7/8" high (open)

FALL DINNER PARTY
INVITATION & COORDINATING THANK YOU NOTE

SUPPLY LIST: Sizzix® Dies Large Squares, Small Pumpkin **Paper** Little Sizzles™ Paper Pad "Pastels", "Watercolors" and "Earth Tones" by Sizzix™ **Miscellaneous** Magic Mesh by Avant' CARD, Raffia, Scissors, Black Micron Pen .03 by Sakura, Xyron Adhesive, Pop Dots by All Night Media, Glue Dots

Tip: Place Magic Mesh onto white cardstock. Die-cut into largest Square on Squares die. Mat with black cardstock. If desired, cut several Pumpkins in each of the orange patterns. Cut them apart at the perforation lines and combine different patterns. Use a Pop Dot to raise the center portion of each Pumpkin.

Alternative Saying:
"For My Little Pumpkin"

Actual Size:
THANK YOU
1-3/4" wide x 1-1/2" high

Actual Size:
INVITATION 6-7/8" wide x 5" high

Thanks for coming!

Actual Size:
INVITATION
3-3/4" x 3-3/4"
THANK YOU
5-1/2" wide x 5-1/4" high

JOIN US
INVITATION
LOVED SEEING YOU
COORDINATING THANK YOU NOTE

SUPPLY LIST: Sizzix® Dies Large Square #1, Small Snowflake, Leaf Trio, Flowers **Paper** Color Wheel™ Bitty Pad "French Country", "And Summer Too", "Flamingo Pink", "Tropical Sun", "Lime Sherbet", "Coral Reef" and "Sunflower" by Provo Craft®, Black Cardstock **Miscellaneous** Chalk by Craf-T Products, Sewing Machine and White Thread, White Fibers by Scrappin' Essentials, Magnet, Black Micron Pen .02 by Sakura, Glue Pen by Zig, Glue Dots

Tip: To make the center flower, just layer two Snowflakes on top of one another, and rotate the top one a bit. **Tip:** What a nice way to remind friends that you've enjoyed their company. The excess waste from the card turns into a "Loved Seeing You" Frame! Just trim the sides down, add a mat of black cardstock and you're good to go. Make it into a fridge magnet by gluing a magnet on the back.

20

BRIDAL SHOWER UMBRELLA
INVITATION & COORDINATING THANK YOU NOTE

SUPPLY LIST: Sizzix® Dies Large Umbrella, Medium Gifts **Paper** Little Sizzles™ Paper Pad "Earth Tones", "Rainbow" and "Country" by Sizzix™ **Miscellaneous** Clear Alphabitties™ "Wrought Iron Black" by Provo Craft®, Pink Embroidery Floss by DMC, Scissors, Black Micron Pen .03 by Sakura, Xyron Adhesive

Tip: Make the Umbrella from very sturdy cardstock so it will hold up the card. Reinforce if necessary. Separate the floss to 'hang' the presents from the Umbrella. Be sure to hide the tape.

Actual Size:
INVITATION 4-1/8" wide x 4-1/8" high (standing)
THANK YOU 2" wide x 2-1/8" high

BRIDAL SHOWER FOR LISA
INVITATION & COORDINATING THANK YOU NOTE

SUPPLY LIST: Sizzix® Die Medium Hearts Primitive **Paper** Pathways "Illuminations" Scrap Pad "Romance" by Provo Craft®, Color Wheel™ Scrap Pad "Avocado" by Provo Craft®, Brown Corrugated Paper **Miscellaneous** Clear Pathways™ Alphabitties™ "Heartland Green" by Provo Craft®, Green Raffia, Tiny Brass Brads, Scissors, Black Micron Pen .03 by Sakura, Xyron Adhesive

Tip: If you find cutting on the fold leaves you with a shape that is flat on one side, just cut one extra shape and adhere it on top of the shape that is cut on the fold.

Alternative Use:
This is a super versatile card that could be used for just about anything!

Actual Size:
INVITATION 4-1/4" wide x 5-1/2" high
THANK YOU 3-1/2" wide x 4-3/8" high

Chapter
Four

CELEBRATING FRIENDSHIP

THINKING OF YOU
GET WELL SOON
I'M SORRY
FRIENDSHIP

CELEBRATING FRIENDSHIP

After a particularly exhausting day raising my two year old twin boys, I received a card in the mail from my best friend and confidant of over twenty years. Inside, I found a photo of my head, glued to a picture of Wonder Woman flying through the air. The caption inside read, "Faster than a speeding stroller, able to leap over mounds of laundry in a single bound, able to change two diapers at the blink of an eye, able to fit a double pram through revolving doors, look up in the sky, it's a bird, it's a plane, no, it's wonderDes!" Knowing that my friend felt that way about me gave me the infectious belief that I really could do it all! I was incredibly fortified like no breakfast cereal could! I was encouraged as even Dr. Dyer had never been able! I had a friend who believed in me, and there is no greater gift. We all can pass on these little treasures of support, kindness, gratitude and yes, even apologies. There is no better time than now, to share some of your soul with someone you love.

Actual Size: 8-1/2" wide x 4-5/8" high

HOPE YOU'RE FEELING BETTER
CARD

SUPPLY LIST: Sizzix® Dies Medium Plant Pots, Small Flower #1, Small Egg **Paper** Little Sizzles™ Paper Pad "Pastels" and "Earth Tones" by Sizzix™, Color Wheel™ Bitty Pad Cardstock "Sherbet" by Provo Craft®, Color Wheel™ Scrap Pad "Azure Blue" by Provo Craft®, Fuzzy Yellow Paper **Miscellaneous** Font: "PC Crazed" (pccrafter.com), Xyron Adhesive

Tip: Try using the large or small Egg dies as leaves. Just fold and chalk, and you've got a great dimensional leaf.

Alternative Use:
This also can be a great Mother's Day card.

BRIGHTER DAYS AHEAD
CARD

SUPPLY LIST: Sizzix® Dies Large Cloud #2, Large Sun **Paper** Little Sizzles™ Paper Pad "Rainbow" by Sizzix™, White Cardstock **Miscellaneous** Chalk by Craf-T Products, Black Micron Pen by Sakura, Xyron Adhesive

Tip: Fold white cardstock into three sections small enough that they don't touch the rule on either side of the Cloud die. Fold right and left sides toward front with sides overlapping (draw a light pencil line in center). Then cut both sheets along pencil line. Write your caption on the sun.

Alternative Sayings:
"To love and be loved is to feel the sun from both sides" (David Viscott)
"Keep your face to the sunshine and you cannot see the shadow" (Helen Keller)

Actual Size: 4-3/4" wide x 4" high

WHENEVER I'M SINKING, I'M SINKING OF YOU
CARD

SUPPLY LIST: Sizzix® Dies Large Doll Body, Large Boy Hair #1, Medium Doll Bath Acccessories, Small Bubbles **Paper** Little Sizzles™ Paper Pad "Watercolors" and "Rainbow" by Sizzix™, Tan Cardstock, Vellum **Miscellaneous** Clear Alphabitties™ "Parlor Black" by Provo Craft®, Clear Alphabet Stickers "Parlor Black" by Provo Craft®, Teal Ultra Foil by Reynolds, Black Micron Pen .05 by Sakura, Xyron Adhesive

Tip: Position Doll's legs and arms to look like they're bending at the elbows and knees. The Doll's ear becomes his nose when you put "side-view" hair on him.

Actual Size: 5" wide x 3-1/2" high

WE'LL MISS YOU
CARD

SUPPLY LIST: Sizzix® Dies Large Car Front, Large Doll Body, Large Doll Boy Hair #1, Large Doll Girl Hair #1, Large Squares, Small Bitty Swimsuit (Bow) **Paper** Color Wheel™ Cardstock Pad "Sherbet", "Tropical" and "Crayon Box" by Provo Craft®, Little Sizzles™ Paper Pad "Watercolors", "Earth Tones" and "Classics" by Sizzix™, Flesh Cardstock **Miscellaneous** Alphabitties™ "Black Fat Dot" by Provo Craft®, Black Micron Pen .02 by Sakura, Xyron 510 Adhesive

Tip: Fold one sheet of lime green paper back to back. Now fold in half again. Place this double folded sheet under die just a little inside the right side of the Car Front. (Make sure that the rest of the die shape has paper completely covering it.) Fold your sunflower yellow paper back to back before cutting the smallest square on the Squares die. You'll need to cut four of these, (cut on the fold). Before adhering the lime sheets together (back to back), slip the circles in between and adhere in place for your headlights. Cut off the steering doll's hands by rounding around the wrists and cutting off the pinky finger. Place hands in front of the wheel. Place Dolls in the very back of the card in back of steering wheel.

Actual Size: 4" wide x 4" high

WISH YOU WERE HERE
CARD

SUPPLY LIST: Sizzix® Die Medium Camera **Paper** Little Sizzles™ Paper Pad "Pastels", "Classics" and "Watercolors" by Sizzix™ **Miscellaneous** Chalk by Craf-T Products, 1/8" Circle Punch by Emaginations, Bead Chain (steal it from your bathtub!), Scissors, Black Micron Pen .03 by Sakura, Xyron Adhesive

Tip: Use your digital camera to click a quick "waving picture" or even tuck a Bitty Body or two in to wave at the card's recipient! Use the white inner portion of the card to help hold the chain in place after punching holes to poke it through.

Alternative Sayings:
"I miss you so much I 'shutter'!"
"We click together like no one else I know"
"Picture us together forever"
"I shutter remembered your birthday"

Actual Size:
2-1/2" wide x 1-7/8" high (folded)

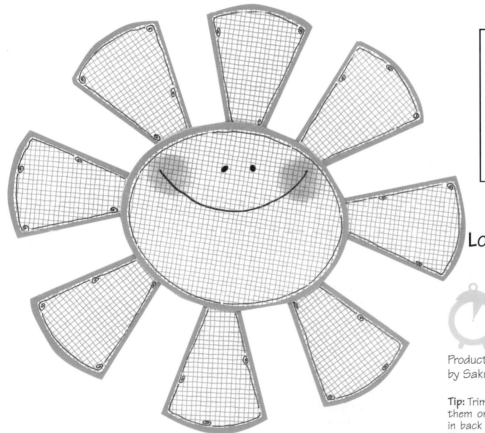

LOOK ON THE SUNNY SIDE
CARD

SUPPLY LIST: Sizzix® Dies Large Scalloped Oval Frame, Small Megaphone **Paper** Color Wheel™ Paper "Tropical Sun" by Provo Craft® **Miscellaneous** Chalk by Craf-T Products, Scissors, Black Micron Pen .05 by Sakura, Xyron Adhesive

Tip: Trim the handles off the Megaphones and place them onto Tropical Sun Cardstock. Slip the ends in back of the cut out portion of the Oval Frame. Place this 'sun' on Tropical Sun Cardstock and trim around to form a border. Draw little lines with swirlies around the face and rays of your sun.

Actual Size: 7-1/8" wide x 6-5/8" high

UNDER THE WEATHER
CARD

SUPPLY LIST: Sizzix® Dies Large Umbrella, Large Hearts, Medium Sand or Snow Mound, Medium Splats **Paper** Little Sizzles™ Paper Pad "Watercolor", "Earth Tones" and "Pastels" by Sizzix™, Bitty Gone Big™ "It's Raining, It's Pouring" and "Country Sky" by Provo Craft® **Miscellaneous** Pathways™ Alphabitties™ "Sepia" by Provo Craft®, Black Micron Pen .05 by Sakura, Glue Pen by Zig, Xyron Adhesive

Tip: When layering a die-cut, sometimes it's easiest to cut out all three colors that you want to use at once. Then trim along the perforation lines of the top layers and placing them on top of the bottom base layer. Lining each different section with a darker color pen provides contrast and definition even when the colors are similar.

Alternative Sayings:
 "Hope you're feeling better soon"
 "Showering you with hugs and kisses"

Actual Size: 5-1/4" wide x 6-1/8" high

YOU'RE MY HERO
CARD

SUPPLY LIST: Sizzix® Die Medium Sand or Snow Mound **Paper** Little Sizzles™ Paper Pad "Earth Tones" by Sizzix™, Color Wheel™ Bitty Pad "Apple Red" by Provo Craft®, Tan Cardstock, Green Vellum **Miscellaneous** Clear Alphabitties™ "Pixie Serif" by Provo Craft®, Glue Pen by Zig

Tip: Tear the brown cardstock to look like meat. Crinkle the green vellum to look like lettuce. Secure the insides of the sandwich (feel free to add your favorite goodies) to the bottom "roll" on the fold and secure to the back of the card so that you can open up the top. It would also be fun to use this as a party invitation and have a few little heads above the sandwich with their hands holding it. Each head could even open up for the what, where and when particulars!

Alternative Sayings:
"Lettuce be Friends Again!"
"Please join us for food, games and fun!"

Actual Size: 3-3/4" wide x 1-1/2" high (folded)

26

JUST FLUTTERING BY
TAG CARD

SUPPLY LIST: Sizzix® Dies Large Tags, Medium Butterfly #3, Medium Grass **Paper** Little Sizzles™ Paper Pad "Rainbow" by Sizzix™, Bitty Scrap Pad "Tropical Colors", "Primary Colors" and "French Country Colors" by Provo Craft® **Miscellaneous** Fun Foam, Raffia, Metallic Embroidery Thread, Scissors, Black Micron Pen .03 by Sakura, Xyron Adhesive

Tip: Cut the Butterfly out of foam and paper, then adhere the paper Butterfly to the foam using the Xyron Machine.

Alternative Sayings:
"You Make My Heart Flutter"
"You wing the prize for the cutest birthday girl!"
"I flutter what you're up to!"

Actual Size: 1-3/4" wide x 3-7/8" high (folded)

BUNCHES OF LOVE
FLOWER BASKET
CARD

SUPPLY LIST: Sizzix® Dies Large Basket, Small Flower #1, Small Leaf Trio **Paper** Little Sizzles™ Paper Pad "Earth Tones" by Sizzix™, Color Wheel™ Cardstock Pad "Sherbet", "Crayon Box" and "Antique" by Provo Craft® **Miscellaneous** Clear Alphabitties™ "Wedge Black" by Provo Craft®, Chalk by Craf-T Products, Art Accentz™ "Black Micro Beedz™" by Provo Craft®, Plaid Ribbon, Art Accentz™ "Terrifically Tacky Tape™ Sheets" by Provo Craft®, Glue Pen by Zig

Tip: To make this card a little easier, cut back to back nutmeg cardstock on the fold so that you have two Baskets in the front and two Baskets in the back. This way, you can place the Flowers between the two front Baskets and between the two back Baskets. This will make the backs look a little more finished and also secure the Tacky Tape Sheets in place.

I love the look of chalked edges of flowers. It also gives them wonderful dimension when you bend the edges up just a little to look like real flowers.

Actual Size:
3-1/4" wide x 4-1/2" high

I TREASURE OUR FRIENDSHIP
CARD

SUPPLY LIST: Sizzix® Die Small Seashell #2 **Paper** Little Sizzles™ Paper Pad "Watercolors" by Sizzix™, Pink Vellum **Miscellaneous** White Pearl Iridescent Fabric Paint by Polymark, Thin Twine, Ribbon, Scissors, Glue Dots, Glue Pen by Zig, Xyron Adhesive

Tip: Make a "pearl" by placing a blob of Iridescent Fabric Paint on a piece of paper and let sit overnight. Practice until you get just the right "pearl" size and shape. Place this "pearl" into the folded Shell on the front. I love the softness and romance that this creates in a card. **Tip:** Dip the edges of this card into water and tear gently to create soft edges.

Actual Size: 4-1/2" wide x 5-1/2" high

FRIENDSHIP IS A SHELTERING TREE
CARD

SUPPLY LIST: Sizzix® Dies Large Green Tree, Medium Grass, Medium Picket Fence **Paper** Little Sizzles™ Paper Pad "Classics", "Earth Tones" and "Pastels" by Sizzix™ **Miscellaneous** Alphabitties™ "Scrapbook White" by Provo Craft®, Glue Pen by Zig, Xyron Adhesive

Tip: Xyron the green sheet of cardstock and the green patterned sheet of paper back to back. Fold these two sheets and cut just to the inside of the right side of the tree top part of the Tree. Place folded green leaves shape onto brown cardstock Tree. Place Tree behind Picket Fence and Picket Fence behind Grass. Don't you just love these quick and easy ones? **Tip:** Try this variation that adds a few minutes: Cut another tree top and separate each of the perforated portions from each other. Back these portions in the green cardstock. Now place each of them on the front of the tree top, overlapping here and there.

Actual Size: 4" wide x 5" high

28

SORRY I DROPPED THE BALL
CARD

SUPPLY LIST: Sizzix® Die Medium Baseball Gear **Paper** Little Sizzles™ Paper Pad "Pastels", "Earth Tones" and "Country" by Sizzix™, Pathways™ Scrap Pad "Heartland" by Provo Craft® **Miscellaneous** Clear Alphabitties™ "Wrought Iron Red" by Provo Craft®, Red Writer Pen by Zig, Black Micron Pen .02 & .05 by Sakura

Actual Size: 3-1/2" wide x 4-1/2" high

Actual Size: 4" wide x 4-1/2" high

I BLEW IT
CARD

SUPPLY LIST: Sizzix® Dies Large Wood Sign, Medium Grass **Paper** Little Sizzles™ Paper Pad "Rainbow", "Earth Tones" and "Watercolors" by Sizzix™, Bitty Gone Big™ "By the Seashore" by Provo Craft® **Miscellaneous** Alphabitties™ "Black Upper and Lowercase Block" by Provo Craft®, Tiny Gold Brads, Black Micron Pen .03 by Sakura, Brown Zig Writer Pen, Xyron Adhesisve

29

IN THE DOG HOUSE
CARD

SUPPLY LIST: Sizzix® Dies Medium Grass, Large Squares, Small Dog **Paper** Bitty Gone Big™ "Dad's Plaid" by Provo Craft®, Little Sizzles™ Paper Pad "Country", "Watercolors" and "Earth Tones" by Sizzix™, Color Wheel™ Bitty Scrap Pad "Caribbean Blue" by Provo Craft® **Miscellaneous** Clear Alphabitties™ "Wedge" "Crayon Box" and "Wedge White" by Provo Craft®, Chain by Teeny Weeny Key Chain Album (use the chain from the album) by Provo Craft®, Black Micron Pen .02 by Sakura, Pop Dots by All Night Media, Glue Pen

Tip: Cut out an extra ear and leg and use Pop Dots to pop up over the existing ear and leg on the Dog.

Alternative Saying:
"I know I'm in the dog house"

Actual Size: 3-1/2" wide x 3-3/4" high

SORRY I WAS A HEEL
CARD

SUPPLY LIST: Sizzix® Die Small Tennis Shoe **Paper** Little Sizzles™ Paper Pad "Pastels" by Sizzix™, Bitty Scrap Pad "Ocean Blue" by Provo Craft®, Designer Paper "Zany Zoo Grass" by Provo Craft® **Miscellaneous** Clear Alphabet Stickers "Parlor Black" by Provo Craft®, Twine, Scissors, Black Micron Pen .03 by Sakura, Glue Pen by Zig, Pop Dots by All Night Media, Xyron Adhesive

Alternative Saying:
"I know you can go the distance"

Actual Size: 3-3/8" wide x 4" high

OOPS I DID IT AGAIN
CARD

SUPPLY LIST: Sizzix® Dies Large Doll Body, Large Girl Hair #1 **Paper** Little Sizzles™ Paper Pad "Rainbow", "Country" and "Watercolors" by Sizzix™, Flesh Cardstock **Miscellaneous** Clear Alphabitties™ "Wrought Iron Black" by Provo Craft®, Chalk by Craf-T Products, Black Wire by Artistic Wire, Wire Pliers, Wire Cutters, Black Micron Pen .02 by Sakura, Xyron Adhesive

Tip: Try cutting the pants lower toward the crotch to make hip huggers. Hand cut the microphone.

Actual Size:
4" wide x 4-1/4" high

Actual Size: 5-3/4" wide x 10" high

EATING CROW
CARD

SUPPLY LIST: Sizzix® Dies Large Scroll, Medium Bat **Paper** Color Wheel™ Bitty Scrap Pad "Apple Red" by Provo Craft®, Little Sizzles™ Paper Pad "Pastels" and "Watercolors" by Sizzix™, Pathways™ Scrap Pad "Heartland" by Provo Craft®, Bitty Gone Big™ "It's Raining, It's Pouring" by Provo Craft®, Tan Cardstock **Miscellaneous** Clear Alphabet Stickers "Parlor Black" by Provo Craft®, Clear Alphabitties™ "Parlor Black" by Provo Craft®, Chalk by Craf-T Products, Scissors, Black Micron Pen .03 by Sakura, Xyron Adhesive

SORRY YOU CAUGHT THE BUG
CARD

SUPPLY LIST: Sizzix® Dies Large Tags, Small Handprint, Small Ladybug **Paper** Little Sizzles™ Paper Pad "Watercolors" by Sizzix™, Color Wheel™ Cardstock Pad "Crayon Box" and "Apple Red" by Provo Craft® **Miscellaneous** Clear Alphabitties™ "Pixie Serif Black" by Provo Craft®, Black Craft Wire by Artistic Wire, Wire Cutters by Artistic Wire, Wire Pliers by Artistic Wire, Thin Red Ribbon, Hole Punch, Scissors, Black Micron Pen .03 by Sakura, Glue Dots, Xyron Adhesive

Tip: Cut the Handprint on the fold at the wrist. This will let you open up the little fingers to show a personal message inside the hand. It is fun to have the hand "holding" the caught Ladybug! Use a glue dot to secure the wire antennae behind the Ladybug's head.

Actual Size: 2" wide x 4" high

GET WELL SOON Rx BOTTLE
CARD

SUPPLY LIST: Sizzix® Dies Large Jar & Label, Large Hearts, Small Jelly Bean **Paper** Little Sizzles™ Paper Pad "Earth Tones" by Sizzix™, Bitty Gone Big™ "Country Sky", "Pink Lady" and "Speckled Frog" by Provo Craft®, Vellum **Miscellaneous** Clear Alphabitties™ "Parlor Black" by Provo Craft®, Scissors, Black Micron Pen .03 by Sakura, Xyron Adhesive

Tip: Cut the vellum on the fold at the top. Cover the top portion with the Label acting as the lid. Line each of the Jelly Beans so that they're more visible through the vellum. Line the outer edges of the vellum Jar on the inside and the outside.

Alternative Sayings:
"Take two jelly beans and call me in the morning" – Attached to a bag of gourmet jellybeans.
    "Sweets for the Sweet"

Actual Size: 3" wide x 4-1/2" high

HEARD YOU CAUGHT THE BUG
CARD

SUPPLY LIST: Sizzix® Dies Medium Grass, Small Frog, Small Dragonfly **Paper** Little Sizzles™ Paper Pad "Watercolors" by Sizzix™, Black Shiny Paper, Vellum **Miscellaneous** Clear Alphabitties™ "Wedge White" by Provo Craft®, Clear Alphabet Stickers "Parlor White" by Provo Craft®, Fuchsia Ultra Foil by Reynolds, Googly Eyes, Black Fabric Covered Wire, Black Micron Pen .03 by Sakura, Glue Pen by Zig, Xyron Adhesive

Tip: Make tufts of Grass with the Grass die. Layer vellum, foil and then vellum to make the Dragonflies look like they are flying.

Alternative Sayings:
'Sorry to hear you've been draggin"
"Hope you're up and buzzing around in no time!"

Actual Size: 5" wide x 3-1/2" high

GET WELL SOON
CARD

SUPPLY LIST: Sizzix® Dies Large Tags, Large Rectangle #1 **Paper** Bitty Gone Big™ "Pink Lady", and Speckled Frog" by Provo Craft®, Color Wheel™ Bitty Pad "Tangerine" by Provo Craft®, 8-1/2 x 11 Black Cardstock **Miscellaneous** Alphabitties™ "Parlor Black" by Provo Craft®; Fibers by On The Surface; Pink, Green and Orange Rick Rack; Glue Dots

Tip: Apply the Rick Rack to folded paper and the die will cut through the paper and Rick Rack, leaving straight edges on the top and bottom. **Tip:** Trim down the Tag to make smaller tags. **Tip:** This card can have a vertical or horizontal orientation.

Actual Size: 4-3/8" wide x 3-1/2" high

33

Chapter
Five

CONGRATULATIONS

CONGRATULATIONS

Many women I know don't celebrate their accomplishments: "Oh, it was nothing" or "It's just my job", they'll say. These amazing women are truly mavericks, yet they down play each credit as if it didn't matter. Some of them work, others raise families, and most of them never feel as though what they're doing is "enough", and to add to that, the daily tasks of many of us become "undone" each and every day. Let's help one another to celebrate even the little accomplishments whatever the achievement, big or small, it is up to us to take the lead, discover them and lend our support. Let all those you love know that YOU believe their accomplishments are real and valid. Whether it's a big event like a new job or career or the birth of a new baby or just a "you did it!", it almost always represents a lot of hard work, tenacity and dedication. Sending any sort of congratulatory card is truly like sending a pat on the back in the mail. It feels really good.

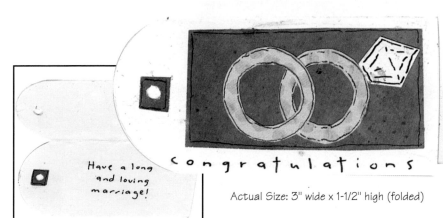

Actual Size: 3" wide x 1-1/2" high (folded)

CONGRATULATIONS
TAG CARD

SUPPLY LIST: Sizzix® Dies Large Circles, Large Tags **Paper** Little Sizzles™ Paper Pad "Pastels" by Sizzix™, Scrap Pad "Let's Hit the Road" by Provo Craft®, Bitty™ Scrap Pad "Dots, Squiggles & Speckles" by Provo Craft® **Miscellaneous** Craft Knife, Scissors, Black Micron Pen .01 by Sakura, Xyron Adhesive

Tip: Use the smallest circle from the Circles die for the rings. Just cut out the centers of each with a craft knife or tiny scissors.

WITH THIS RING
CARD

SUPPLY LIST: Sizzix® Dies Large Circles, Medium Plant Pots, Small Dove **Paper** Bitty Scrap Pad "Love is Everything" by Provo Craft®, Little Sizzles™ Paper Pad "Pastels" by Sizzix™, White Textured Cardstock **Miscellaneous** Font: "PC Casual" Never A Dull Moment PC HugWare™ CD by Provo Craft®, Brown and Perle "Rochaille" Seed Beads by Westrim, Gold Wire by Artistic Wire, Grey Chalk by Craf-T Products, Burgundy Ribbon by Offray, Gold Brads from Target, Oval Punch, 3 Real Twigs about 1" long, Scissors, Pop Dots by All Night Media, Pop Up Glue Dots and Xyron Adhesive

Tip: Place a gold brad in the center of each Pot, folding the ends of the brad sideways to make the pots sturdier. Glue the green Circles to the folded Circles. Randomly glue several Perle "Rochaille" beads on top of the green paper, making sure that some slightly overlap the edge of the Circles. Adhere the Pots to the card using Pop Dots. Adhere the sticks under the Pots using Glue Dots. Make two tiny gold rings by twisting gold wire around a marker or fat pencil. Loop a 2" length of ribbon through the rings and adhere (doubled over) with a Glue Dot. Lightly chalk the right wing of one of the white textured Doves. Trim the second white textured Dove along the perforated line made by the die. Adhere the trimmed Dove over the chalked Dove with a Pop Dot. Trim the beak from tan cardstock and glue it over the beak of the trimmed white textured Dove. Glue a seed bead "eye" on the Dove.

Actual Size: 7-1/2" wide x 5-1/2" high

OVAL DAISY
CARD

SUPPLY LIST: Sizzix® Dies Large Scallop Oval Frame, Small Daisy #1 **Paper** Color Wheel™ Scrap Pad "Sunflower" by Provo Craft®, Bitty™ Scrap Pad "Primary Colors" by Provo Craft®, Vellum, Mulberry Paper **Miscellaneous** Clear Alphabitties™ "Wedge Black" by Provo Craft®, Chalk by Craf-T Products, Canvas, Thin Yarn for Ribbon, Eyelets, Eyelet Setting Tool, Hammer by Simple Ideas, Scissors, Black Micron Pen .03 by Sakura, Xyron Adhesive

Actual Size: 5-3/8" wide x 4-5/8" high

FROM THIS DAY FORWARD
CARD

SUPPLY LIST: Sizzix® Dies Small Flower #1, Medium Leaf, Stem **Paper** Scrap Pad "Wedding Day" by Provo Craft®, Little Sizzles™ Paper Pad "Pastels" by Sizzix™, Color Wheel™ Bitty Scrap Pad "Hydrangea" by Provo Craft®, Light and Dark Green Cardstock **Miscellaneous** Clear Micro Beads by Magic Scraps, Chalks by Craf-T Products, Coluzzle® Card Template by Provo Craft®, Scissors, Sheer White Ribbon, Black Zig Writer, Art Accentz™ "Terrifically Tacky Tape™ Sheets" by Provo Craft®, Xyron Adhesive

Tip: Use Coluzzle® Card and Envelope Template to cut out the card background and trim pink patterned paper about 1/8" all the way around and glue it to your card background. Cut several centers of the Flowers from a Terrifically Tacky Tape™ Sheet. Peel off one side of the backing and dip into your beads. Note: When using large beads sometimes it helps to press your tape sheet into glitter to fill in the holes around the beads.

Actual Size: 5" wide x 7" high

THREE HEARTS ON RIBBON STEMS
CARD

SUPPLY LIST: Sizzix® Die Medium Hearts Primitive **Paper** Color Wheel™ Paper "Sunflower Yellow", "Lilac Petals", and "Hydrangea" by Provo Craft®, White Cardstock **Miscellaneous** Raffia, Metallic Ribbon, Metal Buttons

Tip: Cut hearts on the fold. **Tip:** Make a loop with the metallic thread to close the Heart. Be sure to glue it to the back of the Heart.

Alternative Saying:
"Love you lots!"

Actual Size: 4-1/4" wide x 5-1/2" high

GRADUATION ANNOUNCEMENT
CARD

SUPPLY LIST: Sizzix® Dies Large Jelly Frame, Large Doll Body, Large Doll Boy Hair #1, Medium Doll Graduation, Medium Confetti **Paper** Color Wheel™ Scrap Pad "Caribbean Blue" by Provo Craft®, Little Sizzles™ Paper Pad "Watercolors", "Pastels" and "Classics" by Sizzix™, Flesh Cardstock **Miscellaneous** Clear Alphabitties™ "Blue Pixie Serif" by Provo Craft®, Tiny Gold Brads, Clear Page Protector, Chalks by Craf-T Products, Scissors, Black Micron Pen .03 by Sakura, Xyron Adhesive

Tip: Cut the Jelly Frame on the fold. Cut the page protector just a little larger than the inside of the Jelly Frame. Adhere page protector to back of Jelly Frame. Xyron patterned paper back to back. Adhere folded patterned paper to back of Jelly Frame, just a little wider than the page protector. Leave the top open for now. Insert dressed Doll with diploma glued to his hand and loose confetti between page protector and patterned blue paper. Seal top. Close "shaker" frame and back with solid blue cardstock. Apply your message inside the card with the clear blue Alphabitties™. This also works well for a graduation announcement.

Actual Size: 4-5/8" wide x 5" high

Actual size is 3-3/4" wide x 4-3/4" high

YOUR CAREER IS REALLY MOVING!
CARD

SUPPLY LIST: Sizzix® Dies Large Car Front, Large Rectangle Frame **Paper** Little Sizzles™ Paper Pad "Classics" and "Earth Tones" by Sizzix™, Bitty Scrap Pad "Simply School" and "Primary Colors" by Provo Craft® **Miscellaneous** Font: "PC Ratatat" A Gathering of Friends PC HugWare™ CD by Provo Craft®, Scissors, Xyron Adhesive

Tip: Die-cut and decorate the Car Front first, then add to the front of the Rectangle Frame on the fold. Trim off the side of the Car that hangs over the edge with your scissors.

Alternative Sayings:
"Congratulations on your Promotion!"
"Have Fun on your Trip!"
"We'll Miss You!" (We're Moving Announcement)

SLAM DUNK
CARD

SUPPLY LIST: Sizzix® Dies Small Basketball **Paper** Color Wheel™ Cardstock Scrap Pad "Crayon Box" by Provo Craft® **Miscellaneous** Clear Alphabitties™ "Wedge Crayon Box" by Provo Craft®, Plastic Mesh, Scissors, Black Micron Pen .03 by Sakura, Pop Dots by All Night Media, Xyron Adhesive

Tip: Place the Basketball on a Pop Dot. Place the mesh "basket" on two sets of two Pop Dots, stacked on top of each other. This will create the dimension of the Basketball going into the basket. Line with your black pen on top of the perforation lines on the Basketball. This is the perfect card to use to congratulate someone on a sporting accomplishment. Feel free to substitute other sporting shapes that fit your recipient's interests. Sizzix® also cuts plastic mesh beautifully. Try cutting out shapes like Stars, Hearts and Frames and cross-stitching your own Christmas ornaments!

Alternative Sayings:
"Swoosh"
"Nothin' but Net!"
"You're the Man!"
"Congratulations on the Big Win!"

Actual size: 4-7/8" wide x 6-1/8" high

CONGRATS ON YOUR NEW CAR
CARD

SUPPLY LIST: Sizzix® Dies Medium Car, Small Bitty Doll, Small Bitty Girl Hair #1, Small Bitty Dresses **Paper** Little Sizzles™ Paper Pad "Watercolors" and "Earth Tones" by Sizzix™ **Miscellaneous** Alphabitties™ "Parlor Black" by Provo Craft®, Eyelets and Fibers by Scrappin' Essentials, Chalks by Craf-T Products, Sakura Gelly Roll Pens

Tip: Flowing hair is cut freehand.

Alternative Sayings:
"Welcome to the Fast Lane"
"Heard You're Shifting Gears—Good Luck in Your New Job"
"Cruisin' on to another year"
"You have amazing drive!—Good luck in your new location"

Actual Size 3-1/8" wide x 2-1/2" high

Actual Size: 2-3/4" wide x 3" high (folded)

CONGRATULATIONS ON BUILDING YOUR OWN HOME
CARD

SUPPLY LIST: Sizzix® Die Medium Hammer & Nail **Paper** Black Cardstock, Silver and Copper Metallic Paper **Miscellaneous** Alphabitties™ "Wedge White" by Provo Craft®, Black Micron Pen by Sakura

Alternative Saying:
"You've hit the nail on the head!"

CONGRATULATIONS ON YOUR NEW JOB
CARD

SUPPLY LIST: Sizzix® Dies Fun Serif Uppercase "I", Small Cloud #1, Large Train Engine, Medium Road & Wavy Border, Medium Grass, Large Doll Body, Large Doll Overalls, Large Doll Girl Hair #1 **Paper** Little Sizzles™ Textures "Sandbox", "Summer Earth" and "Leather" by Sizzix™; Little Sizzles™ Paper Pad "Pastels" and "Classics" by Sizzix™; Bitty Gone Big Paper "When the Wind Blows" by Provo Craft® **Miscellaneous** Alphabitties™ "Black Wedge" by Provo Craft®, Tiny Gold Brads, Chalk by Craf-T Products, Black Micron Pen .08 by Sakura, Glue Pen by Zig, Glue Dots

Tip: To make the girl's arm wave the sign, just cut an extra long arm out, and attach it underneath her shirt with a Bradletz™. **Tip:** Use the Uppercase "I" to make the handle for the sign. **Tip:** Use the Road & Wavy Border to make the train tracks by placing thin strips of black cardstock across the tracks.

Actual Size: 5" wide x 6-3/4" high

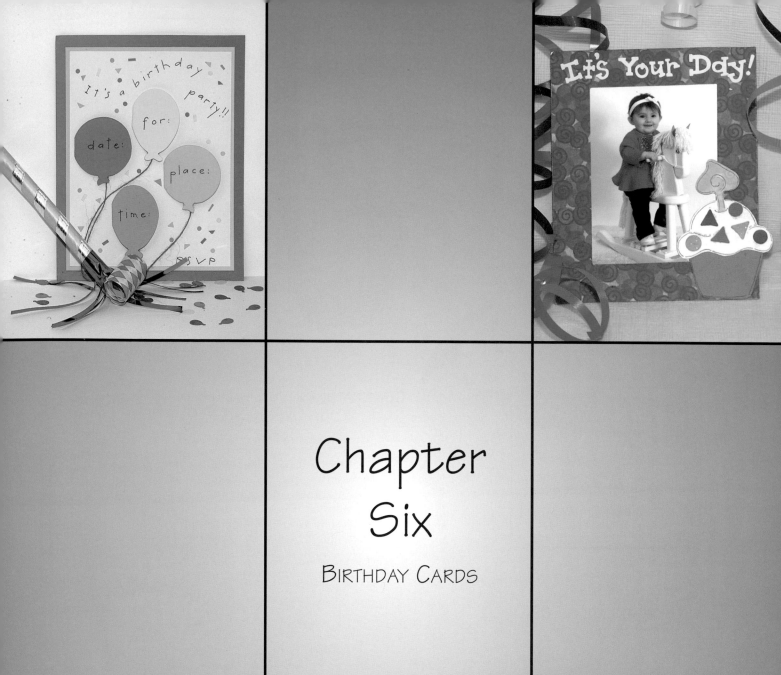

Chapter
Six

Birthday Cards

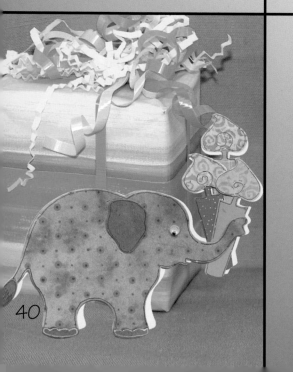

BIRTHDAY CARDS

Our Birthday – The one day out of every year that belongs to each of us. A card received on this day reminds us that we're loved, remembered and that there's no one just like us! It's a little snippet that we can tuck in our back pocket and take with us for the rest of the year! Mark your calendars and let your loved ones know you remember.

Actual Size: 1-3/4" wide x 3-3/4" high

ELISE'S BIRTHDAY INVITATION
TAG

SUPPLY LIST: Sizzix® Dies Large Tags, Medium Candles **Paper** Little Sizzles™ Paper Pad "Pastels" by Sizzix™, Scrap Pad "Country Fall" by Provo Craft®, Bitty Scrap Pad "Tropical" by Provo Craft® **Miscellaneous** Scissors, Black Micron Pen .03 by Sakura, Xyron Adhesive

Tip: Place Candle on the Tag after cutting the Tag and then trim off the Candle bottom. This same Tag can be used as the thank you note that you send to your guests after the party. My daughter and I have found that making the tags and cards together can be one of the most rewarding events before and after a birthday party.

HAPPY BIRTHDAY DINOSAUR
CARD AND TAG

SUPPLY LIST: Sizzix® Die Large Squares **Paper** Little Sizzles™ Paper Pad "Pastels" and "Classics" by Sizzix™, Bitty Gone Big™ "Lost in the Woods" and "Forever Green" by Provo Craft® **Miscellaneous** Clear Alphabitties™ "Wrought Iron Black" by Provo Craft®, Clear Letters "Wrought Iron Black" by Provo Craft®, Vellum Sticker "Prehistoric Park" by Provo Craft®, Chalk by Craf-T Products, Scissors, Black Micron Pen .03 & .08 by Sakura, Xyron Adhesive

Tip: Draw swirly lines around the Squares to mimic the lettering style. For the To/From Tag: Back the larger dinosaur with white cardstock for stability. Cut little 'tufts' of grass to go in front and in back of him.

Alternative Uses:
This could easily be used for a Dinosaur Birthday Party Invitation.
The To/From Tag could be the Thank You Notes that you and your son send out to all of his little friends.

Actual Size:
GIFT TAG
3-3/4" wide x 3-1/2" high

Actual Size: CARD 8-1/4" wide x 4-5/8" high

41

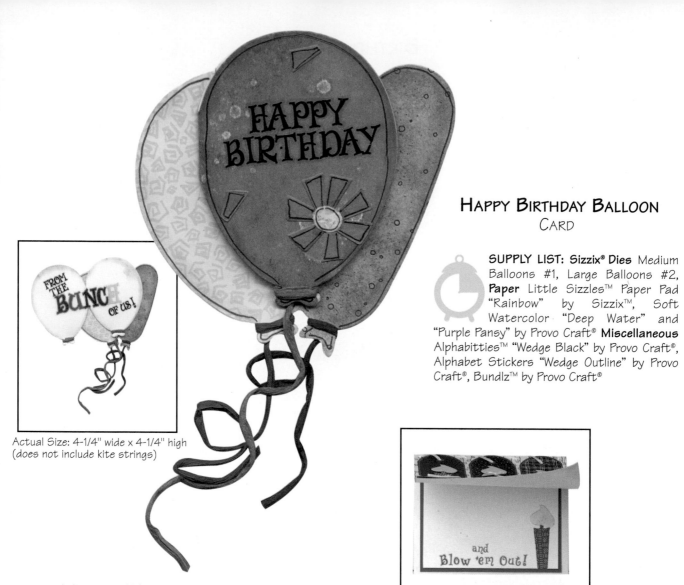

HAPPY BIRTHDAY BALLOON
CARD

SUPPLY LIST: Sizzix® Dies Medium Balloons #1, Large Balloons #2, **Paper** Little Sizzles™ Paper Pad "Rainbow" by Sizzix™, Soft Watercolor "Deep Water" and "Purple Pansy" by Provo Craft® **Miscellaneous** Alphabitties™ "Wedge Black" by Provo Craft®, Alphabet Stickers "Wedge Outline" by Provo Craft®, Bundlz™ by Provo Craft®

Actual Size: 4-1/4" wide x 4-1/4" high
(does not include kite strings)

MAKE A WISH AND
BLOW 'EM OUT
CARD

SUPPLY LIST: Sizzix® Dies Large Tags (use smallest tag), Medium Candles **Paper** Little Sizzles™ Paper Pad "Pastels" by Sizzix™, Color Wheel™ Scrap Pad "Caribbean Blue" by Provo Craft®, Color Wheel™ Cardstock "Crayon Box" by Provo Craft® **Miscellaneous** Clear Alphabitties™ "Wedge Red" by Provo Craft®, Thin White Ribbon, Hole Punch, Glue Dots , Xyron 510 Adhesive

Tip: After cutting out your blue Tags, mat them with red solid paper for a nice contrast. Leave a bit of the Candle bottom "hanging" off the bottom of the Tags, then trim Candle bottom even with Tag bottom for a contemporary look. Weave ribbon through holes on top of card to finish off this birthday card.

Actual Size: 5-1/2" wide x 4-1/4" high

42

LOOK WHO'S FOUR
TAG

SUPPLY LIST: Sizzix® Dies Large Tags, Large Doll Body, Large Doll Boy Hair #1 **Paper** Little Sizzles™ Paper Pad "Rainbow" by Sizzix™, **Miscellaneous** Alphabet Beads, Clear Alphabitties™ "Red Wedge" by Provo Craft®, Eyelets by Doodlebug, Ribbon by Offray, Wire by Artistic Wire, Black Micron Pen .005 by Sakura

Tip: For a finished look to the inside of this card, adhere eyelets, torn paper and wrap wire with alphabet beads before Xyroning the inside layer of blue paper.

Actual Size: 1-3/4" wide x 3-7/8" high (not including boys head)

Actual Size: 7" wide x 7-7/8" high

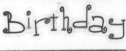

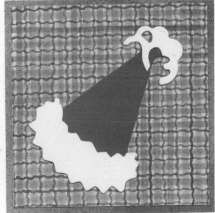

4 SQUARE HAPPY BIRTHDAY
CARD

SUPPLY LIST: Sizzix® Dies Medium Party Hat, Medium Candles, Medium Party Favor, Medium Gifts **Paper** Little Sizzles™ Paper Pad "Earth Tones" and "Rainbow" by Sizzix™, White Cardstock **Miscellaneous** 12" Paper Trimmer, Xyron Adhesive

Tip: Place each birthday shape onto the large Square shape. Mat with coordinating yet contrasting colors. Trim on your paper trimmer.

Alternative Saying:
Substitute any Birthday wish here.

HAPPY BIRTHDAY LITTLE BUG
CARD

SUPPLY LIST: Sizzix® Dies Large Circles, Medium Confetti **Paper** Little Sizzles™ Paper Pad "Watercolors" by Sizzix™, Bitty Gone Big™ "Cross Your Heart" and "Sweetheart Speckles" by Provo Craft® **Miscellaneous** Clear Alphabitties™ "Pixie Serif Black" by Provo Craft®, Circle Hole Punch by Provo Craft®, Googly Eyes, Black Fabric Covered Wire, Wire Cutting Tool, Wire Pliers, Scissors, Black Micron Pen .01 by Sakura, Glue Dots, Xyron Adhesive

Alternative Saying:
"Sorry you caught the bug."

Actual Size: 5-1/8" wide x 3-5/8" high

DID YOU THINK I'D FORGET ABOUT YOUR BIRTHDAY?
CARD

SUPPLY LIST: Sizzix® Dies Large Elephant, Medium Candles **Paper** Little Sizzles™ Paper Pad "Watercolors" by Sizzix™, Bitty Scrap Pad "Dots, Squiggles & Speckles" by Provo Craft®, Bitty Color Wheel™ Scrap Pad "Calypso Green" and "Flamingo Pink" by Provo Craft®, Bitty Gone Big™ "Marine Reef" by Provo Craft® **Miscellaneous** Scallop Paper Shaper Scissors by Provo Craft®, Googly Eyes, Scissors, Black Micron Pen .03 by Sakura, White Gel Pen by Marvy, Pop Dots by All Night Media, Xyron Adhesive

Tip: You can use a Scallop Paper Shaper Scissor to make the Elephant's toenails. Try lining them with a white gel pen. I'm convinced that googly eyes make everything just a little bit cuter. Pick them up in several sizes, but I use the smallest size the most.

Alternative Sayings:
"Did you think I'd forget about your birthday?"
"I remembered!"
"Sorry I forgot your birthday"

Actual Size: 5" wide x 4-1/4" high

ANOTHER YEAR OLDER!
CARD

SUPPLY LIST: Sizzix® Dies Medium Stars Primitive, Small Moon **Paper** Little Sizzles™ Paper Pad "Watercolors" by Sizzix™ **Miscellaneous** Clear Alphabitties™ "Wrought Iron Black" by Provo Craft®; Coluzzle® Card & Envelope Template, Cutting Mat, and Guarded® Swivel Knife by Provo Craft®; Sheer Yellow Ribbon by Offray; Chalk by Craf-T Products; Eyelets by Doodlebug; Eyelet Setting Tool; Hammer by Simple Ideas; Scissors; Black Micron Pen .03 by Sakura; Pop Dots by All Night Media, Xyron Adhesive

Tip: Trim two lengths of ribbon about 12 inches long. Xyron green cardstock and adhere back to back to the checked paper, while tucking the ribbon between the layers on both of the long ends of the paper. Fold the card in half to make sure that the ribbon lengths are even. Now unfold, and cut the diagonal window out with your Coluzzle® Card Template. Save the cut out square and place it in the window with a Pop Dot as shown. Place a Pop Dot under your Moon for some added dimension. Bone folders work wonderfully when you have several layers to fold or you'd like a sharp fold. Try using this as a baby announcement or baby shower invitation!

Alternative Saying:
"When you reach for the moon, you'll catch the stars"

Actual Size: 3-1/4" wide x 4-1/2" high

IT'S YOUR DAY
MAGNET CARD

SUPPLY LIST: Sizzix® Dies Large Rectangle Frame, Medium Ice Cream Cone, Medium Candles **Paper** Color Wheel™ Paper Pad "Calypso Green", "Tropical Sun", "Flamingo Pink" and "Acapulco Purple" by Provo Craft®, Little Sizzles™ Paper Pad "Earth Tones" and "Pastels" by Sizzix™ **Miscellaneous** Alphabitties™ "Scrapbook White" by Provo Craft®, Scissors, Black Micron Pen .03 by Sakura, Xyron Magnetic Sheets

Tip: This is a wonderful way to give a gift that keeps on giving! By running the Rectangle Frame through the Xyron Magnetic Sheets, you can create a refrigerator magnet that you can slip a photo underneath. Leave it up for the entire year! Everyone will be surprised to find their smiling face under the frame on their special day. It'd be fun to include a picture of you and the birthday boy or girl behind the frame as they open the card. Make the cupcake by trimming down the Ice Cream Cone. The top scoop will become the icing!

Alternative Sayings:
"Happy Birthday!"
"Congratulations!"
"Another Year Older!"

Actual Size: 4-7/8" x 4"

It's Your Day!

HAPPY BIRTHDAY SON
CARD

SUPPLY LIST: Sizzix® Die Small Dragonfly **Paper** Scrap Pad "Fish All Day" by Provo Craft®, White Cardstock, Vellum **Miscellaneous** Font: "A Gathering of Friends" PC Zesty PC HugWare™ CD by Provo Craft®; Coluzzle® Circle Template, Card & Envelope Template, Cutting Mat, and Guarded® Swivel Knife by Provo Craft®; Googly Eyes; Scissors; Black Micron Pen .03 by Sakura; Glue Dots, Hermafix Transfer Dots; Xyron Adhesive

Tip: This is a "manly" birthday card for an older son, father, brother or grandfather – especially one who likes the great outdoors. Add dimension to the Dragonflies by slightly folding up the vellum wings. Googly eyes make the Dragonflies look like the real thing! If you're not handy with a computer or can't find a font that you like, try using Alphabitty stickers to write the message on the card's front.

Alternative Sayings:
"Happy Father's Day"
"Thanks for taking us Fishing!" or "Camping!"

Actual Size: 7" wide x 5" high

FLOWER IN THE WINDOW
CARD

SUPPLY LIST: Sizzix® Die Large Daisy #2 **Paper** Color Wheel™ Paper Pad "Spring Green", "Aquamarine", "Lime Sherbet", "Pumpkin" and "Tangerine" by Provo Craft® **Miscellaneous** Coluzzle® Card and Envelope Template, Cutting Mat, and Guarded® Swivel Knife by Provo Craft®; Eyelets by Doodlebug; Eyelet Setting Tool; Hammer by Simple Ideas; Fiber; Black Micron Pen .03 by Sakura; Xyron Adhesive

Alternative Saying:
You can put any saying in this card.

Actual Size: 5" wide x 7" high

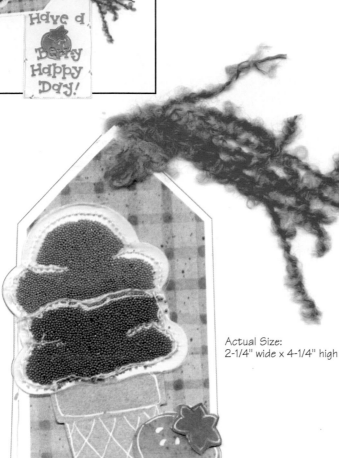

HAVE A BERRY HAPPY BIRTHDAY
CARD

SUPPLY LIST: Sizzix® Dies Large Tags, Medium Ice Cream Cone, Medium Berries (available Fall 2003) **Paper** Little Sizzles™ Paper Pad "Pastels" and "Earth Tones" by Sizzix™, Bitty Gone Big™ "Stained Grass" and "Pink Lady" by Provo Craft®, White Cardstock **Miscellaneous** Fibers by Scrappin' Essentials, Art Accentz™ "Green and Pink Micro Beedz™" by Provo Craft®, Page Protector by C-Thru, White Gel Roller by Marvy, Embosser by Chatterbox, Sewing Machine, White Thread, Scissors, Funnel, Glue Dots, Xyron Adhesive

Tip: Die-cut one Ice Cream Cone using white cardstock. This will be your base. Fold page protector in half and cut with Ice Cream Cone die. Trim off the cone section. Sew both layers together around the bottom scoop, leaving a small space. Add green Micro Beedz™ between layers using a funnel. Sew up the small space. Repeat this step using the pink Beedz™ on the top scoop. Place on top of your white layer. Add a brown cone underneath.

Actual Size:
2-1/4" wide x 4-1/4" high

SENDING FLURRIES OF BIRTHDAY WISHES YOUR WAY!
CARD, ORNAMENT OR TAG

SUPPLY LIST: Sizzix® Die Large Snowman **Paper** Little Sizzles™ Textures "Sandbox" by Sizzix™, Little Sizzles™ Paper Pad "Watercolors" by Sizzix™ (nose) **Miscellaneous** Primitive Heart Bradletz™ by Provo Craft®, Dotlets by Doodlebug, Chalk by Craf-T Products, Buttons by Dress It Up, Page Protector by C-Thru, White Floss by DMC, Red Fabric by Moda, Hammer by Simple Ideas, Bundlz Wired Raffia by Provo Craft®, Eyelet Setter, Needle, Glue Pen by Zig and Glue Dots

Tip: To make the bag, just hand or machine sew with white floss, and fill with snowflake buttons.

Actual Size:
3-3/8" wide x 4-3/8" high

47

Chapter Seven

Notes To Kids

NOTES TO KIDS

When I was a little girl, my Mom often tucked a little note into my lunch box. My mother was a single mom and worked full time, so these notes weren't fancy, in fact, they were usually written on a napkin and contained some small encouragement or just "I Love You". She always put a little happy face in the "o" that she would sign in "Love, Mom". I still remember the feeling that those notes brought to me. They gave me an almost giddy sense of confidence throughout the day. I knew that I was loved, even if I had disobeyed, or had missed the throw at first during baseball practice. It was a reminder that I had a home base and that I was safe.

Actual Size: 5-1/8" wide x 5-1/2" high

I BEE-LEAF 'N EWE
CARD

SUPPLY LIST: Sizzix® Dies Large Bare Tree, Small Leaf Trio **Paper** Bitty Gone Big™ "Country Sky" by Provo Craft®, Little Sizzles™ Paper Pad "Earth Tones" by Sizzix™, Color Wheel™ Cardstock "Antique Palette" and "Crayon Box Palette" by Provo Craft® **Miscellaneous** Clear Alphabitties™ "Parlor Black" and "Nativity" by Provo Craft®, "Meadow" Build-A-Series Stickers by Provo Craft®, Paper Trimmer, Xyron Adhesive

Tip: Xyron Country Sky paper back to back and fold to make the base of your card. Cut three of the Leaf Trios on the fold (from the top). These will open up to reveal your message.

Alternative Sayings:
Any rebus message will work in this card format. Take a look at all of your spare stickers and come up with a fabulous message to inspire and delight your little ones. Note: This is also really fun to send to adults. I love trying to figure out the message that lies within pictures. Be careful not to get to intricate with your messages though, I once sent my Mom a Mother's Day card that said, "Happy (picture of a moth), 'er's' Day" and she didn't get it.

STAR STUDENT
NOTE

SUPPLY LIST: Sizzix® Die Large Star #1 **Paper** Color Wheel™ Paper Pad "Sunflower Yellow" by Provo Craft®, Little Sizzles™ Paper Pad "Watercolors" by Sizzix™ **Miscellaneous** Clear Alphabet Letters "Parlor Black" by Provo Craft®, Clear Alphabitties™ "Parlor Black" by Provo Craft®, Scissors, Black Micron Pen .02 by Sakura, Xyron Adhesive

Tip: After cutting the Star on the fold, just back with black cardstock and trim around the star shape for a contrasting background that really makes the star pop!

Alternative Sayings:
"You make the grade!"
"You're my shining star!"
"When I wished upon a star, I got you!"

Actual Size: 4-1/2" wide x 4-3/8" high

YOU CAN DO IT
NOTE

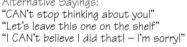

SUPPLY LIST: Sizzix® Die Large Jar & Label **Paper** Little Sizzles™ Paper Pad "Pastels" by Sizzix™, Color Wheel™ Cardstock "Apple Red" by Provo Craft® **Miscellaneous** Clear Alphabitties™ "Wedge Red" by Provo Craft®, Silver Foil by Reynolds, Embossing Tool or Stylus, Scissors, Black Micron Pen .05 by Sakura, Glue Dots, Xyron Adhesive

Tip: Use your embossing tool or stylus to make the "ridges" and "lid" of your can by putting gentle pressure and dragging at the same time. I like "The Embosser" by Chatterbox. To make the "lid", just trim the top of the Jar into an oval and stick on top of the Jar. Sometimes with a tough material to attach like foil, Glue Dots really come in handy. They stick just about any thing to just about anything! Use the Label on the Jar die to cut both the red and white labels, then trim the white one down a bit. Attach white on top of red and you've got a label for your message!

Alternative Sayings:
"CAN't stop thinking about you!"
"Let's leave this one on the shelf"
"I CAN't believe I did that! – I'm sorry!"

Actual Size: 2-3/4" wide x 3-3/8" high

HOGS & KISSES
NOTE

SUPPLY LIST: Sizzix® Dies Large Jar & Label, Small Double Heart, Small Pig **Paper** Color Wheel™ Scrap Pad "Hydrangea" by Provo Craft®, Little Sizzles™ Paper Pad "Pastels" and "Watercolor" by Sizzix™ **Miscellaneous** Silver Foil by Reynolds®, Clear Alphabitties™ "Wedge Sherbet" by Provo Craft®, Clear Page Protector, Embossing Tool or Stylus, Scissors, Black Micron Pen .02 by Sakura, Hermafix® Dots

Tip: Cut off the bottom portion of the Double Heart die to make the "kisses". Glue the white cardstock strip onto the back of the "kiss" and seal with another "kiss" on the back. I popped these into my little girl's lunch sack one day and she was all smiles as she got off the bus. **Tip:** Page protectors are really tough to get to stick together. On these I used Hermafix Dots to secure the side and top. It helps if you use the natural bottom and side fold of the protector to make up the bottom and side of your card. This way, you only have to secure the top and one side of your card. You can also sew the edges together by hand or machine.

Alternative Sayings:
"Sweets for the Sweet"
"This Little Piggy gets to go on a 'Mommy-Daughter Date' tonight!"

Actual Size: 2-3/4" wide x 4" high

THANKS FOR GOING THE EXTRA MILE
CARD

SUPPLY LIST: Sizzix® Dies Medium Road & Wavy Border, Medium Car, Medium Grass, Small Bitty Body, Small Bitty Boy Hair #1, Small Bitty Shorts & Top, Small Bitty Overalls **Paper** Color Wheel™ Paper Pad "Tropical" by Provo Craft®, Little Sizzles™ Paper Pad "Earth Tones" and "Classics" by Sizzix™, Bitty Scrap Pad "Kid's Stuff" by Provo Craft®, Flesh Cardstock **Miscellaneous** Clear Alphabitties™ "Wedge White" by Provo Craft®, Silver Eyelets by Doodlebug, Medium Circle Punch, Black Micron Pen .03 by Sakura, Xyron Adhesive

Tip: Even though your Car doesn't need to be on the fold, its easier to place two Tropical Sun sheets back to back when you die-cut the Car. This way, you can slip the Bitty Body in between the Cars and the front and back both look finished. Also slip the circle punched black circles in between the front and back Car. Place a silver eyelet in the center as a hubcap. Trim off the brim of the Bitty Overalls Hat and round the corners. Adhere it sideways under the Hat. Cut little "tufts" from the Grass die to line the bottom of this card.

Actual Size: 4" wide x 3-3/4" high

APPLE OF MY EYE
NOTE

SUPPLY LIST: Sizzix® Die Small Apple **Paper** Bitty Gone Big™ "Cross Your Heart" by Provo Craft®, Little Sizzles™ Paper Pad "Earth Tones" by Sizzix™, Color Wheel™ Bitty Scrap Pad "Ivory Coast" and "Spring Green" by Provo Craft® **Miscellaneous** Clear Alphabitties™ "Parlor White" and "Black" by Provo Craft®, Scissors, Black Micron Pen .08 by Sakura, Xyron Adhesive

Tip: Trim the Ivory Coast paper a little smaller than the apple shape and line the inside of the Apple. Draw little "seeds" around "of my eye".

Alternative Sayings:
"Seedless to say, I adore you!"
"For my little bookworm"
"I find you very a-pealing!"

Actual Size: 1-5/8" wide x 2" high (folded)

ICE CREAM WITH SPRINKLES
CARD

SUPPLY LIST: Sizzix® Die Medium Ice Cream Cone **Paper** Bitty Scrap Pad "Ivory Coast", "Hydrangea" and "Azure Blue" by Provo Craft®, Embossed Tan Cardstock **Miscellaneous** Font: "Beach" Little Images PC HugWare™ CD by Provo Craft®, Beads, Liquid Adhesive by Tombow, Bond 527 Multi-Purpose Cement

Tip: For a crumpled look crumple your cardstock, then flatten out before die-cutting. **Tip:** If you use your computer to type out the saying, make sure it is only about 1" wide and 1-1/2" high.

Alternative Sayings:
"Here's the Scoop"
"You're the Best!"

Actual Size: 2" wide x 3-1/8" high

YOU'RE MY SUNSHINE
CARD

SUPPLY LIST: Sizzix® Dies Large Sun; Large Cloud #2; Medium Swirls, Multi **Paper** Color Wheel™ Bitty Pad "Tropical Sun" by Provo Craft®, White Cardstock **Miscellaneous** Alphabitties™ "Scrapbook Yellow" by Provo Craft®", Chalk by Craf-T Products, Scissors, Black Micron Pen .03 by Sakura, Xyron Adhesives

Tip: Can you imagine the feeling of joy that your recipients will feel knowing that they brighten your day? Try giving this card to your child and watching them glow. After cutting the Cloud on the fold, cut the Sun on the fold as well and slip it between the folded layers of the Cloud. Don't forget to add a solid yellow Swirl in the center of the Sun.

Alternative Sayings:
"You Brighten My Day"
"There are Sunny Days Ahead"
"The Forecast calls for Sunny Weather!"

Actual Size: 4-3/4" wide x 3-1/2" high (folded)

HEAR YE, HEAR YE
NOTE

SUPPLY LIST: Sizzix® Die Large Scroll **Paper** Little Sizzles™ Paper Pad "Classics" by Sizzix™ **Miscellaneous** Pathways Sepia Alphabitties™ by Provo Craft®, Chalk by Craf-T Products, Scissors, Brown Zig Writer

Tip: I've found that my children often respond well to written notes posted on locations such as the television or their bedroom door. It helps to remind them of their obligations so that I don't need to. Feel free to personalize the message to fit your family's needs.

Alternative Sayings:
Placed on the fridge –
"Please clean up your snacks when you're finished"
Placed on the bathroom mirror in the bathroom –
    "Teeth that are white are Mom's delight!"
"Brushing teeth after you eat, gives your smile a
    well deserved treat"

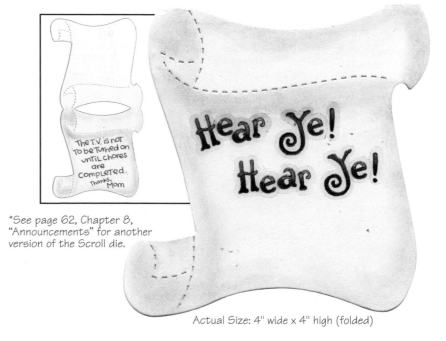

*See page 62, Chapter 8, "Announcements" for another version of the Scroll die.

Actual Size: 4" wide x 4" high (folded)

Actual Size:
5-1/2" wide x 8-1/2" high

I LIKE YOU
CARD

SUPPLY LIST: Sizzix® Dies Large Stars, Small Frog **Paper** Little Sizzles™ Paper Pad "Pastels" and "Watercolors" by Sizzix™, Scrap Pad "Happy Halloween" by Provo Craft® **Miscellaneous** Avery® Shipping Labels, Black Beads, Black Embroidery Floss by DMC, Googly Eyes, Scissors, Black Micron Pen .03 by Sakura, Xyron Adhesive

Tip: Try sewing on the googly eyes instead of gluing if you want them to be super secure. Avery® shipping labels worked great here to save time on cutting and gluing. Print the words of the title on the lower half of your shipping label. Fold label in half, with the printing on the inside of the label. Die-cut a Frog with the fold just under the Frog's eyes, making sure that the printing falls on the belly of the Frog when the die-cut label is flipped up. Peel the backing off the label and stick the purple Frog to the assembly on the green rectangle and adhere. The fold will flip up at the Frog's mouth to reveal the message!

Alternative Sayings:
"You're the Top Frog!"
"You make my heart leap!"

Actual Size:
3-1/4" wide x
4-1/2" high

BEST FISHES
NOTE

SUPPLY LIST: Sizzix® Dies Either Large Award OR Large Trophy, Small Fish **Paper** Bitty Gone Big™ Paper "Marine Reef" by Provo Craft®, Color Wheel™ Scrap Pad "Flamingo Pink", "Calypso Green", "Tropical Sun" and "Ivory Coast" by Provo Craft® **Miscellaneous** Pathways Alphabitties™ "Traditional Black" and "Multi" by Provo Craft®, Scissors, Black Micron Pen .02 by Sakura, Xyron Adhesive

Tip: Cut one Award or Trophy out of the Marine Reef paper as well as the Ivory Coast Cardstock. Use this as your circle or pattern for your "fishbowl" in the center of either die-cut. Trim "layers" in Marine Reef to let the Fish "swim" through. Try drawing around the edges with wavy or broken lines to give these notes a "watery" feel. I also outlined the Fish and waves to separate them.

Alternative Sayings:
"I 'fish' you a Happy Birthday"
"Fishing you a Wonderful Day!"
"You're a Real Catch!"
"I'm glad I caught you"

Actual Size: 3-1/8" wide x 4-5/8" high

53

GOOD LUCK IN SCHOOL
CARD

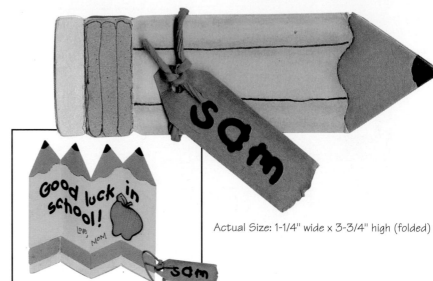

SUPPLY LIST: Sizzix® Die Medium Pencil **Paper** Little Sizzles Paper Pad "Watercolor" and "Earth Tones" by Sizzix™, Color Wheel™ Paper Pad "Tropical Sun" and "Hydrangea" by Provo Craft® **Miscellaneous** Alphabitties™ "Black Fat Dot" by Provo Craft®" Apple Sticker by Provo Craft®, Chalk by Craf-T Products, Raffia, Scissors, Black Micron Pen .03 by Sakura, Xyron Adhesive

Tip: Accordion fold paper twice and die-cut. Attach extra folded sections with adhesive. Use the yellow layer as your base, and add the other color embellishments on top. **Tip:** Lining with a black pen and chalking really makes this card stand out.

Alternative Sayings:
"You're Sharp!"
"You've got the WRITE stuff"
"Pencil me in for a date tonight"

Actual Size: 1-1/4" wide x 3-3/4" high (folded)

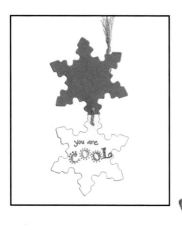

YOU ARE COOL
CARD

SUPPLY LIST: Sizzix® Die Small Snowflake **Paper** Color Wheel™ Scrap Pad "Liberty Blue" by Provo Craft®, Silver Foil **Miscellaneous** 1/16" Hole Punch by McGill, Mini Snowflake Punch by Marvy Uchida, Alphabet Stamps by Hero Arts, Black Ink, Blue Gelly Roll Pen by Sakura, Embossing Powder by Stampin' Up, Embroidery Floss by DMC, Xyron Adhesive

Tip: Remember to Xyron the papers back to back before folding and die-cutting.

Alternative Sayings:
"I'm Sorry I was a Flake"
"You're the Coolest"
"There's a warm hug waiting at home for you!"

Actual Size: 1-3/4" wide x 1-3/4" high

I LOVE YOU
BOOKMARK

SUPPLY LIST: Sizzix® Dies Large Daisy #2 **Paper** Bitty Scrap Pad "Tropical" by Provo Craft® **Miscellaneous** Fibers by On The Fringe, White Eyelet by Doodlebug, Eyelet Setter, Hammer by Simple Ideas, Circle Punch by Marvy Uchida, Chalks by Craf-T Products, Coluzzle® Rectangle Template by Provo Craft®, Zig Writer Pens, Tape Runner

Tip: Cut the Daisy on the fold of the three petals. Circle punches work well for the centers of the flowers.

Alternative Sayings:
"You Go Girl"
"My Best Buds"
"Spring Has Sprung"

Actual Size: 3" wide x 7-3/4" high

WHEN YOU WISH UPON A STAR
BOOKMARK

SUPPLY LIST: Sizzix® Dies Large Tags, Medium Primitive Stars **Paper** Bitty Scrap Pad "Nature Works" by Provo Craft®, Metallic Paper **Miscellaneous** Sheer Ribbon, Wire by Artistic Wire, Brad

Tip: Cut off tip of tag.

Actual Size:
2-1/4" wide x
3-3/4" high

FALL LEAVES
BOOKMARK

SUPPLY LIST: Sizzix® Dies Small Leaf #4, Small Leaf #1, Small Leaf #1 Tiny **Paper** Color Wheel™ Cardstock Scrap Pad "Nature Palette" and "Crayon Box Palette" by Provo Craft®, Sage Cardstock, Burlap Paper by Carolee's Creations **Miscellaneous** Twine, Scissors, Black Micron Pen .03 by Sakura, Xyron Adhesive, Pop Dots by All Night Media

Tip: Spritz various colors of cardstock with water and crumple them up. Flatten them out and allow to dry completely. Cut out the bookmark with the burlap paper. Adhere Leaves to the front of the bookmark, placing some of them on Pop Dots for dimension. Autumn is a time to sit back, relax and enjoy the beautiful colors. It's also a nice time to enjoy the calm surrounding and curl up with a good book!

Alternative Sayings:
"Autumn is a second spring when every leaf is a flower" ~ Albert Camus,
"Everyone must take time to sit and watch the leaves turn" ~ Elizabeth Lawrence,
"Be-leaf in yourself!"

Actual Size:
2-1/2" wide x 8" high

LAUGH, LOVE, SMILE, DREAM, HOPE
BOOKMARK

SUPPLY LIST: Sizzix® Die Large Tags **Paper** Pathways Scrap Pad "Illuminations" by Provo Craft®, Vellum **Miscellaneous** Font: "PC Kennedy" Fontmania PC HugWare™ CD by Provo Craft®, Silver Eyelet by Doodlebug, Eyelet Setting Tool, Fibers by Art Sanctum, Embossing Powder by Stampin' Up, Black Micron Pen .05 by Sakura, Xyron Adhesive

Tip: Write or use your computer to convey the message in the papers "bubbles". This is a super way to tell your child you love them while encouraging them to read, read, read! This bookmark would also be fun to give to someone on their graduation day.

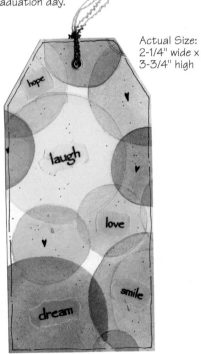

Actual Size:
2-1/4" wide x
3-3/4" high

DAISY
BOOKMARK

SUPPLY LIST: Sizzix® Dies Large Daisy #2 **Paper** Pathways Scrap Pad "Illuminations" by Provo Craft®, Little Sizzles™ Paper Pad "Pastels" by Sizzix™ **Miscellaneous** Chalk by Craf-T Products, Paper Shapers "Medium Wave" by Provo Craft®, Swirl Punch by Family Treasures, Circle Punch by Darice, Fibers by Art Sanctum, Hole Punch, Black Micron Pen .03 by Sakura, Xyron Adhesive

Tip: Cut out bookmark shape from pink cardstock and using Wavy Paper Shapers, cut off the top edge. Chalk lightly with pink chalk around the edges. Use green fibers to make the stems and sew them into the cardstock with a needle. Try using a bookmark instead of a card to add to a gift for someone.

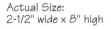

Actual Size:
3-3/8" wide x
6-1/2" high

55

Chapter
Eight

ANNOUNCEMENTS

ANNOUNCEMENTS

Sometimes you're so excited about some news you'd like to shout it from the rooftops! Other times, you'd just like to softly share a wonderful secret. A small card on the fold will announce your news with flair! Pop a few in the mail next time something great happens – your friends will be happy to hear from you!

SMILING BABY
Announcement

SUPPLY LIST: Sizzix® Die Large Circles **Paper** Little Sizzles™ Paper Pad "Pastels" and "Watercolors" by Sizzix™, Bitty Color Wheel™ Scrap Pad "Hydrangea" by Provo Craft® **Miscellaneous** Heart and Square Bradletz™ by Provo Craft®, Sheer Green Ribbon by Offray, Raffia, Paper Shapers "Mini Scallop" by Provo Craft®, Scissors, Black Micron Pen .03 by Sakura, Glue Dots, Xyron Adhesive

Tip: Cut the mouth of the baby by using the smallest circle from the Circles die and trimming into a moon shape. Attach the Bradletz at the bottom of the smile, being careful to place it so that the smile can also turn into a frown by rotating. This gives the card an interactive feel that kids and grown ups alike will have fun with. **Tip:** If your Bradletz™ aren't the color that you'd like, simply heat the top of the design with an embossing tool, then dip into the color of embossing powder that matches your card. Heat with the embossing tool again to 'seal' the color and you're ready to go! NOTE: I like to use Sticker Tweezers by Provo Craft® to hold my Bradletz™ so that I don't burn my fingers.

Alternative Saying:
"We're Overjoyed"

Actual Size: 3-5/8" wide x 3-5/8" high

BABY BLOCKS
ANNOUNCEMENT

SUPPLY LIST: Sizzix® Dies Small Block, Small Fun Serif Uppercase "B", "A", and "Y" **Paper** Little Sizzles™ Paper Pad "Pastels" by Sizzix™, Color Wheel™ Bitty Scrap Pad "Hydrangea" and "Azure Blue" by Provo Craft® **Miscellaneous** Pink Ribbon by Offray, Scissors, Black Micron Pen .03 by Sakura, Glue Dots, Xyron Adhesive

Tip: Use the perforation lines to guide you where to cut when trimming out the fronts and sides of each Block. Remember to cut each Block on the fold at the top. Another neat idea is to put a picture of the new baby in the first or last Block so that friends and family can get a sneak peak of the new little one!

Actual Size: 8-1/4" wide x 4-3/4" high

Actual Size: 3-7/8" wide x 4-7/8" wide

JUMP FOR JOY
ANNOUNCEMENT

SUPPLY LIST: Sizzix® Dies Large Jelly Frame, Small Frog **Paper** Little Sizzles™ Textures "Sandbox" by Sizzix™, Little Sizzles™ Paper Pad "Pastels" by Sizzix™ **Miscellaneous** Alphabitties™ "Wedge Black" by Provo Craft®, Bradletz™ by Provo Craft®, Wiggly Eyes, Wire, Chalks by Craf-T Products

Tip: To highlight this Frog, use black pen to outline and chalk the edges. Coil wire around a pencil for 'spring'.

Alternative Saying:
"Hop on over!"

BABY BOY
ANNOUNCEMENT

SUPPLY LIST: Sizzix® Die Large Sailboat **Paper** Scrap Pad "Let's Hit the Road" by Provo Craft®, Bitty Scrap Pad "French Country" and "Primary Colors" by Provo Craft® **Miscellaneous** Scissors, Black Micron Pen .03 by Sakura, Xyron Adhesive

Tip: Write the baby's name on the front as shown with 's.s' in front of it. Include the birth information on the inside of the card. For a soft stamped look on gift tags or wrapping paper try die-cutting the Sailboat out of compressed sponge. Place sponge under water and then wring fully. Dip into paint to match your card and sponge onto white butcher paper. Let dry and wrap your present with homemade coordinating wrapping paper!

Alternative Saying:
"Our Little Ship has Come In!"

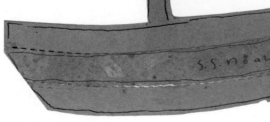

Actual Size: 3-3/4" wide x 3-7/8" high

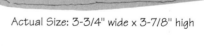

Actual Size: 3-3/4" wide x 3-7/8" high

BABY GIRL
ANNOUNCEMENT

SUPPLY LIST: Sizzix® Die Large Sailboat **Paper** Color Wheel™ Scrap Pad "Hydrangea" by Provo Craft®, Bitty Scrap Pad "Just Ducky Baby" by Provo Craft® **Miscellaneous** Scissors, Black Micron Pen .01 by Sakura, Xyron Adhesive

Tip: Cut the little flower on the sail from the Just Ducky Baby Scrap Pad Paper. Line in black pen. Include the birth information on the inside of the card. Can also be used as a baby gift card!

It's A Girl Clothesline

ANNOUNCEMENT

SUPPLY LIST: Sizzix® Dies Large Doll Overalls, Medium Grass, Small Teddy Bear, Small Bitty Dresses **Paper** Bitty Scrap Pad "Just Ducky Baby", "Fabric Textures", "French Country" and "Pocketful of Posies" by Provo Craft® **Miscellaneous** Twine, Small Clothespins, Scissors, Black Micron Pen .03 by Sakura, Pop Dots by All Night Media, Xyron Adhesive

Tip: This is a super card to mass produce! Invite all of your most supportive friends over to a "baby announcement party". Assign each guest a 'job' (one person die-cuts the clothing and Teddy Bears, another cuts the background and matting pieces, yet another addresses the envelopes, etc.) In no time at all, you've got your announcements done! When the precious bundle arrives, all you have to do is write in the information and you're all set! Serve something easy like dip in a bread bowl and water with citrus slices.

Actual Size 8-1/2" wide x 5-1/2" high

The Stork Has Arrived

ANNOUNCEMENT

SUPPLY LIST: Sizzix® Dies Large Zig Zag Frame, Medium Bird **Paper** Little Sizzles™ Paper Pad "Pastels" by Sizzix™, White & Orange Cardstock **Miscellaneous** Alphabitties™ "Wrought Iron" by Provo Craft®, Black Wiggly Eyes, Chalk, Black Micron Pen by Sakura, Wired Raffia

Tip: Be sure to have the legs hang over the end of the card for a 'quirky look'!

Alternative Saying:
"Welcome...little one!"

Actual Size:
3-1/2" wide x 5-1/4" high (including legs)

HEAR YE!
ANNOUNCEMENT

SUPPLY LIST: Sizzix® Die Large Scroll **Paper** Pathways™ Scrap Pad "Romance" by Provo Craft® **Miscellaneous** Pathways™ Designer Alphabitties™ "Traditional Black" by Provo Craft®, Font: "PC Ratatat" A Gathering of Friends PC HugWare™ CD by Provo Craft®, Chalk by Craf-T Products, Scissors, Brown Zig Writer

Alternative Sayings:
"A Kings Declaration"
"By Royal Decree, it is our pleasure to announce"

Actual Size: 4" wide x 4" high (folded)

MOON & HANGING STAR
ANNOUNCEMENT

SUPPLY LIST: Sizzix® Dies Medium Stars Primitive, Small Moon **Paper** Color Wheel™ Paper Pad "Sunflower" by Provo Craft®, Vellum "Teal" & "Yellow" **Miscellaneous** Bradletz™ by Provo Craft®, Silver Wire by Artistic Wire, Wire Cutting Tool, Paper Trimmer, Black Micron Pen .03 by Sakura, Glue Dots, Xyron Adhesive

Tip: Cut the yellow vellum Moon on the fold from the top so the little wire that the Star hangs from closes the Moon. Secure the wire to the yellow patterned paper with a Glue Dot. Attach the teal vellum to the inside of the card with Bradletz™ on each of the four corners. Write or type your announcement information on the inside vellum.

Alternative Sayings:
"A Star is Born"
"Our Little Moonbeam has arrived"

Actual Size:
2-7/8" wide x
3-1/2" high

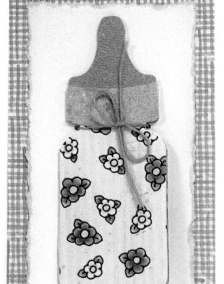

Actual Size: 2-7/8" wide x 4-7/8" high

BABY BOTTLE
ANNOUNCEMENT

SUPPLY LIST: Sizzix® Die Medium Baby Bottle **Paper** Scrap Pad "That's My Baby" by Provo Craft®, Little Sizzles™ Paper Pad "Pastels" by Sizzix™ **Miscellaneous** Font: "PC Casual" Never A Dull Moment PC HugWare™ CD by Provo Craft®, Chalks by Craf-T Products, Fiber, Scissors, Liquid Adhesive by Tombow

Xyron the green paper back to back before folding and die-cutting. Fan fold the green paper and then smooth out to give it the look of the lines on a bottle ring. Tear a white rectangle about 4" long and 2-1/4" wide. Chalk the edges with pink chalk. Poke tiny holes just under the bottle ring on both sides. Thread the fiber under the torn white cardstock and up through each side. Tie fiber around bottle to close.

Alternative Uses:
This card works well as a "Congratulations on your new baby" card, or for a baby shower gift card.

BASEBALL
CARD

SUPPLY LIST: Sizzix® Dies Medium Baseball Gear, Medium Banner, Large Circle #2, Medium Grass **Paper** Color Wheel™ Paper "Apple Red" and "Leaf Green", Paper by Provo Craft® **Miscellaneous** Alphabitties™ "Parlor Red" by Provo Craft®, Red and Black Pen

Tip: Outline the Banner with Apple Red paper. With a red pen, make lines on the Circle to look like a baseball.

Alternative Saying:
"You're A Pro!"

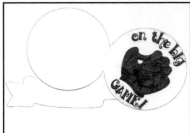

Actual Size:
4-1/4" wide x 3-3/4" high

CONGRATULATIONS ON YOUR NEW HOME
TAG

SUPPLY LIST: Sizzix® Dies Large Tags, Medium Grass **Paper** Pathways™ Scrap Pad "Romance" by Provo Craft®; White, Light Brown, and Green Cardstock **Miscellaneous** Brad, Chalks, Ribbon, Scallop Scissors

Tip: This is a great way to get double duty from your Sizzix® dies–make the Tag into a house!

Alternative Saying:
"We're Moving!"

Actual Size:
2" wide x
3-7/8" high

WE'VE MOOOOVED
ANNOUNCEMENT

SUPPLY LIST: Sizzix® Dies Large Tags, Large Cow, Medium Grass **Paper** Bitty Gone Big™ "It's Raining, It's Pouring" by Provo Craft®, Little Sizzles™ Paper Pad "Primary", "Pastels" and "Watercolor" by Sizzix™ **Miscellaneous** Clear Alphabitties™ "Wedge Black" by Provo Craft®, Chalk by Craf-T Products, Sheer Green Ribbon by Offray, Raffia, Scissors, Black Micron Pen .03 by Sakura, Xyron Adhesive

Tip: For the insides of your Tags, just adhere Grass onto your white cardstock. Fold and die-cut with the Tag Die. **Tip:** Hand cut the spots on the Cow and adhere them where you'd like. Chalk around the edges and perforated lines for a shadowed effect. Place the Cow over the tops of your two Tags sitting one above the other. Trim between them, remembering to let the Cow's muzzle hang over the top Tag. Adhere the backs of the Tags to the front of this card and you've got an utterly wonderful moving announcement!

Alternative Sayings:
"We've Found an Utterly Wonderful New Home!"
"We're Moooving!"

Actual Size: 5-3/4" wide x 4-1/4" high

GRAD BANNER
ANNOUNCEMENT

SUPPLY LIST: Sizzix® Dies Large Doll Body, Medium Doll Graduation, Large Pennant **Paper** Little Sizzles™ Paper Pad "Watercolors" and "Rainbow" by Sizzix™; Black, Flesh and White Cardstock **Miscellaneous** Alphabitties™ "Pixie Serif Black" by Provo Craft®

Tip: To make the arms going up, clip the sleeves and arms and turn the die-cut upside down.

Alternative Sayings:
"You've graduated"
"Congrats"

Actual Size: 5-1/2" wide x 3-3/4" high (folded)

DRAGONFLY
ANNOUNCEMENT

SUPPLY LIST: Sizzix® Dies Small Dragonfly, Large Rectangle #1, Large Squares, **Paper** Soft Watercolor "Pool-Marble Plaid" by Provo Craft®, Green Vellum and White Cardstock by Provo Craft® **Miscellaneous** Alphabitties™ "Wedge White" by Provo Craft®, Alphabet Stickers "Sherbet Pixie Serif" by Provo Craft®, Art Accentz™ "Sparklerz Glitter" by Provo Craft®, Art Accentz™ "Terrifically Tacky Tape™" by Provo Craft®, Art Accentz™ "Beadz™" by Provo Craft®, Bradletz™ by Provo Craft® Scallop Scissors, Chalk by Craf-T Products, Twine

Tip: Crinkle the vellum before adhering it to the card. Use Terrifically Tacky Tape™ when cutting the Dragonfly, remove backing & dip in Beadz™.

Alternative Saying:
"Welcome Spring"

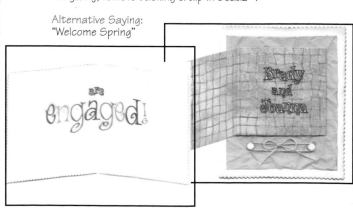

Actual Size: 3-1/2" wide x 4-1/4" high

Praising God for His goodness to us
we, Lori and Kraig
joyously invite you to witness
a celebration of love
when we exchange marriage vows
on Saturday, December thirteenth
nineteen hundred and eighty-six
at one o'clock in the afternoon
Live Oak Church of the Nazarene
Live Oak, California

Reception following ceremony

INTERTWINED HEARTS
ANNOUNCEMENT

SUPPLY LIST: Sizzix® Die Small Double Heart **Paper** Designer Paper "Wedding Bouquet" by Provo Craft®, Little Sizzles™ Paper Pad "Pastels" by Sizzix™, Color Wheel™ Bitty Scrap Pad "Avocado Green" by Provo Craft®, Vellum **Miscellaneous** Chalk by Craf-T Products, Scissors, Xyron Adhesive

Tip: Print out all of your information onto vellum. Now tear and chalk each vellum piece a little smaller than your background mat and front of invitation. **Tip:** Tuck one of the Double Hearts under where it will intertwine with the other so that they look connected.

Actual Size: 5" wide x 7" high

RECTANGLE FRAME
ANNOUNCEMENT

SUPPLY LIST: Sizzix® Dies Large Rectangle Frame, Small Flower #1 **Paper** Little Sizzles™ Paper Pad "Earth Tones" by Sizzix™, Bitty Scrap Pad "French Country" and "Crackled Antiques/Faux Finishes" by Provo Craft® **Miscellaneous** Font: "PC Stone Script" Little Images PC HugWare™ CD by Provo Craft® (using dark blue ink), Scissors, Xyron Adhesive

Tip: Place the Flowers onto the blue paper, then adhere it onto the back of the Rectangle Frame in back of the vellum. This gives the floral background a subdued look. **Tip:** This card will work for any occasion. Try putting a little glitter or confetti in between the vellum and blue paper layer to make your own "shaker" card. You could even try it as a place card!

Alternative Uses:
Works well as an invitation, thank you card, friendship card, etc.

Mr. and Mrs. Brad Young
request the honor of your presence
at the marriage of their daughter

Emily Marie
with
Mr. Kevan Matthews

on Friday, the fourth of July
at four o'clock
at the St. Thomas church
New York

Actual Size: 3-3/4" wide x 4-5/8" high

Chapter Nine

CLASSIC
THANK YOU CARDS

CLASSIC THANK YOU CARDS

I used to buy those big boxes of thank you cards that were all the same. But the more I thought about it, the people that do kind things for me, aren't all the same, and deserve a special thank you just for them. Now I can create a card to thank my daughter's teacher for encouraging her and noticing how hard she is trying in class. Or I can thank my next door neighbor for washing my car with a little green car card that resembles my Volkswagen. I want my thank you cards to reflect my appreciation of the uniqueness of these people.

Actual Size: 4" wide x 2-1/8" high (folded)

THANKS, YOU'RE A LIFE SAVER!
CARD

SUPPLY LIST: Sizzix® Dies Large Doll Body, Medium Wave, Medium Doll Summer Clothes **Paper** Little Sizzles™ Paper Pad "Rainbow" by Sizzix™, Bitty Gone Big™ "Country Sky" by Provo Craft®, Tan Cardstock **Miscellaneous** Chalk by Craf-T Products, Scissors, Black Micron Pen .01 & .05 by Sakura, Xyron Adhesive

Tip: Cut the Wave on the fold at the bottom. **Tip:** Snip off the Girl's hand and adhere it 'waving' at the recipient of this card.

Alternative Sayings:
"Come to my Pool Party!"
"Whenever you're in deep water, call me!"
"Congratulations on passing your Swimming Test"
"Thanks for taking me swimming!"

FOR MY BUS DRIVER
CARD

SUPPLY LIST: Sizzix® Dies Large Bus Back, Small Bitty Doll Body, Small Bitty Boy Hair #1, Small Bitty Girl Hair #1, Small Bitty Shorts & Top, Small Bitty Dresses, Large Stars **Paper** Little Sizzles™ Paper Pad "Watercolors" and "Classics" by Sizzix™, Color Wheel™ Cardstock Scrap Pad "Crayon Box Palette" by Provo Craft®, Scrap Pad "Awesome Athletes" by Provo Craft®, Flesh Cardstock **Miscellaneous** Alphabitties™ "Kid's Black" by Provo Craft®, "Pooh Bear Face" Punch by Family Treasures, Red and Blue Acrylic Jewels by Westrim Crafts, Clear Page Protector by C-Line, Scissors, Black Micron Pen .03 by Sakura, Xyron Adhesive

Tip: It's nice to thank our children's bus drivers now and then for keeping our children safe when transporting them to and from school. At the end of the school year, any bus driver would appreciate this card, possibly along with a gift certificate or present for a job well done **Tip:** This little card can be personalized with your school district's name and/or bus number. You could also match the Bitty Doll's hair and gender to your own children!

Alternative Saying:
"Best Bus Driving Award"

Actual Size: 4" wide x 4-1/2" high

YOU'RE SO KIND
CARD

SUPPLY LIST: Sizzix® Dies Large Jelly Frame, Small Leaf #1, Small Leaf #1 Tiny **Paper** Little Sizzles™ Paper Pad "Earth Tones" by Sizzix™, Color Wheel™ Cardstock Scrap Pad "Nature Palette" and "Sherbet Palette" by Provo Craft®, Vellum **Miscellaneous** Chalks by Craf-T Products, Hole Punch by Provo Craft®, Fibers by On The Surface, Scissors, Black Micron Pen .05 by Sakura, Glue Pen by Zig, Xyron Adhesive

Tip: After cutting the Frame on the fold, use the rub-on wax along the edge. Now fold the vellum in half and cut to size to fit within the Frame. Adhere in the fold to give the card some extra stability. Don't fully adhere the vellum around the edges yet. Punch holes in the Leaves so they will hang in various directions. **Tip:** The message inside is easy. . . just use the cut out from the inside of the Frame and tear the edges. Write the message, rub on color or chalks and adhere.

Alternative Sayings:
"Leaf-ing you is always hard"
"Our time together always 'Leaves' too Quickly"

Actual Size: 4-7/8" wide x 3-7/8" high

THANKS FOR PLANTING SEEDS OF KINDNESS
CARD

SUPPLY LIST: Sizzix® Dies Large Doll Body, Large Doll Girl Hair #1, Large Doll Overalls, Medium Plant Pots, Medium Sunflower, Small Doll Shoes #1, Small Bitty Swimsuit **Paper** Little Sizzles™ Paper Pad "Rainbow", "Pastels" and "Earth Tones" by Sizzix™, Color Wheel™ Scrap Pad "Avocado" by Provo Craft®, Bitty Gone Big™ "Under the Haystack" by Provo Craft®, Flesh Cardstock **Miscellaneous** Clear Alphabitties™ "Wedge Black" by Provo Craft®, Paper Shaper Scissors "Mini Scallop" by Provo Craft®, Raffia, Spanish Moss, Scissors, Black Micron Pen .03 by Sakura, Glue Dots, Xyron Adhesive

Tip: Cut the center of the Sunflower on the fold so that you can write "Thanks" inside the center. Adhere an extra flower center on top of the folded center so that you don't have a flat spot at the top of the center. Draw little dots on the center with your black pen. **Tip:** Use the Doll's feet as socks. For feminine socks, just trim with Mini Scallop Paper Shapers at the tops. **Tip:** To make an overall dress, just trim the Overalls at the crotch line and curve slightly upward on each side. You can also make overall shorts by cutting slightly lower and including the crotch.

Alternative Sayings:
"Thanks, that was big of you"
"My Love Grows for You Everyday"

Actual Size:
4-1/4" wide x
5-1/8" high

THANK YOU AGAIN & AGAIN
CARD

SUPPLY LIST: Sizzix® Die Large Daisy #2 **Paper** Little Sizzles™ Paper Pad "Pastels" by Sizzix™, Color Wheel™ Scrap Pad "Sunflower" by Provo Craft® **Miscellaneous** Vellum Stickers "Hearts & Swirls" by Provo Craft®, White Embroidery Floss by Anchor, Ladybug Button, Green Raffia, Scissors, Black Micron Pen .03 by Sakura, Glue Dots, Xyron Adhesive

Tip: Bend the raffia and secure behind the Daisy to look like leaves. **Tip:** Fold this card each time you'd like to add a word to the message. "Have A Daisy Of A Day" would need two sections folded twice and pieced together. **Tip:** This technique works well with the Large Daisy for a medium sized card, and also the Small Daisy for a diminutive card.

Alternative Sayings:
"Thank you, Thank you, Thank you, Thank you"
"Thanks For All You Do"
"Have a Daisy of a Day"

HEART IN THE WINDOW
CARD

SUPPLY LIST: Sizzix® Dies Large Rectangle #1, Large Rectangle #2, Medium Hearts Primitive **Paper** Little Sizzles™ Paper Pad "Watercolors" by Sizzix™, Pathways Scrap Pad "Romance" by Provo Craft® **Miscellaneous** Pathways Alphabitties™ "Sepia" by Provo Craft®, Sheer Beige Ribbon by Offray, Scissors, Black Micron Pen .03 by Sakura, Xyron Adhesive, Pop Dots by All Night Media

Tip: Use the larger Rectangle #1 for the base of the card, then cut just the front window out using Rectangle #2. Line the card with green paper. Die-cut the Heart on the fold, so that the patterned paper forms the inside of the Heart. Die-cut another Heart to place on top of the Heart on the fold. Express your sentiment inside the Heart with Alphabitties™. Tie ribbon around the Heart, securing the ribbon in the back using the Pop Dots.

Alternative Sayings:
"Heartfelt Thanks"
"I Love You with all my Heart"

Actual Size:
2" wide x 2" high (folded, not including ribbon)

Actual Size:
3-1/2" wide x
4-1/2" high

FLOWER THANK YOU
CARD

SUPPLY LIST: Sizzix® Dies Square #2, Small Flowers **Paper** Little Sizzles™ Textured Handmade Papers "Sandbox" by Sizzix™, Bitty™ Gone Big "Pink Lady" and "Speckled Frog" by Provo Craft®, White Cardstock **Miscellaneous** Heart Bradletz™ by Provo Craft®, Fibers by Scrappin' Essentials, Chalk by Craf-T Products, Sewing Machine, White Thread, Tiny Hole Punch or Scissors, Pink Writer by Zig, Art Accentz™ "Terrifically Tacky Tape™" by Provo Craft®

Tip: Use the smaller Flower as the center of the larger Flower.

Actual Size:
3-1/4" wide x 3-1/4" high

67

FLY FISHING DAD
CARD

SUPPLY LIST: Sizzix® Dies Large Squares, Small Trout **Paper** Little Sizzles™ Paper Pad "Watercolors" by Sizzix™, Bitty™ Gone Big "Blueberry Pie" and "Raffia Wreath" by Provo Craft® **Miscellaneous** Fishing Fly, Scissors, Black Micron Pen .03 by Sakura, Glue Dots, Xyron Adhesive

Tip: Xyron black cardstock to back of Blueberry Pie paper. Fold and cut on the fold with the largest Square shape. Now Xyron Raffia Wreath back to back, fold and cut on the fold at the top of the Trout. Attach the fly on the front of your card with Glue Dots. **Tip:** Write a little note to Dad inside the Trout.

Alternative Sayings:
"I fish you were here"
"You're the catch of a lifetime!"

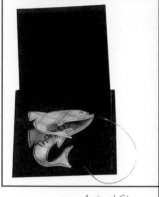

Actual Size:
2-1/4" wide x
2-1/4" high

Actual Size: 4-3/4" wide x 6-5/8" high

THANK YOU MRS. SMITH
CARD

SUPPLY LIST: Sizzix® Dies Large Rectangle #1, Large Rectangle #2, Medium Pencil, Medium Hearts Primitive **Paper** Little Sizzles™ Paper Pad "Watercolors" and "Rainbow" by Sizzix™ **Miscellaneous** Alphabitties™ "Scrapbook White" by Provo Craft®, Chalk by Craf-T Products, Scissors, Black Micron Pen .03 by Sakura, Xyron Adhesive

Alternative Saying:
"I'd give you an A Plus!"

SQUARE FLOWER
THANK YOU NOTE

SUPPLY LIST: Sizzix® Dies Large Daisy #2, Large Squares **Paper** Little Sizzles™ Paper Pad "Pastels" by Sizzix™, Color Wheel™ Cardstock Scrap Pad "Sherbet Palette" by Provo Craft®, Color Wheel™ Scrap Pad "Spring Green" by Provo Craft® **Miscellaneous** Embroidery Floss by DMC, Eyelets by Magic Scraps, Eyelet Setting Tool, Hammer by Simple Ideas, Button, 1/8" Hole Punch, Scissors, Black Micron Pen .03 by Sakura, Glue Dots, Xyron Adhesive

Tip: Fold strip of Spring Green patterned paper in half and cut the largest Square shape on the fold. Cut the next largest Square shape from Custard Cardstock and adhere to inside of card. **Tip:** This is the perfect little tag to go with almost any gift. Just thread floss through the handles of a gift bag or tie to a ribbon on a wrapped box and you're sure to please. **Tip:** Cut a Daisy out of compressed sponge, then paint a bag or wrapping paper to coordinate with your Daisy card.

Actual Size: 2" wide x 2" high

Actual Size:
2" wide x 2" high

LAVENDER HEARTFELT THANKS
CARD

SUPPLY LIST: Sizzix® Dies Large Squares, Medium Hearts Primitive **Paper** Little Sizzles™ Paper Pad "Pastels" by Sizzix™ **Miscellaneous** Paper Shapers Scissors "Mini Scallop" by Provo Craft®, Bradletz™ "White Primitive Heart" by Provo Craft®, Black Micron Pen .02 by Sakura, Xyron Adhesive

Tip: Use your Mini Scallop Paper Shapers to create 'lace' around the Heart. Secure onto the card with a little white heart Bradletz. Draw lines around the Square and Heart with your black pen. **Tip:** Making lots of these cards at a time is simple. You can assembly line cut and glue tons of these in no time!

Alternative Sayings:
"Thank You with All my Heart"
"Lots of Love"

BEADED THANK YOU DAISY
CARD

SUPPLY LIST: Sizzix® Dies Large Daisy #2, Small Leaf Trio **Paper** Little Sizzles™ Paper Pad "Pastels" by Sizzix™ **Miscellaneous** Alphabitties™ "Fat Dot Fun Multi" by Provo Craft®, Art Accentz™ "Micro Beedz™" by Provo Craft®, Magic Mesh by Avant' CARD, Scissors, Black Micron Pen .03 by Sakura, Xyron Adhesive, Art Accentz™ "Terrifically Tacky Tape™ Sheets™" by Provo Craft®

Tip: Adhere Terrifically Tacky Tape™ Sheet onto white cardstock. Cut out all shapes. Pull off the top coating layer. Place your Magic Mesh onto this layer. Dip into Beedz™. Now gently pull off the magic mesh and you'll have a "plaid" pattern on your Daisy. **Tip:** The center and leaves can have this pattern as well, or have solid coverage. Try just making the center plaid and not the Daisy for a fun change.

Alternative Saying:
Any personal message would be appropriate here.

Actual Size: 3-1/2" wide x 3" high

LAVENDER HEART GARLAND
THANK YOU NOTE

SUPPLY LIST: Sizzix® Dies Large Squares, Medium Border Heart **Paper** Little Sizzles™ Paper Pad "Pastels" by Sizzix™ **Miscellaneous** Green Fabric Covered Wire, Scissors, 1/16" Hole Punch, Black Micron Pen .03 by Sakura, Xyron Adhesive, Pop Dots by All Night Media, Glue Dots

Tip: Xyron lavender cardstock. Fold your lavender cardstock back to back before die-cutting so that you have a nice thick shape to lace your wire through. (This will alleviate tearing the paper while threading the wire through the holes.) **Tip:** Line your Heart Border with the black pen before you lace your wire through and adhere it to the card front with a Pop Dot. Secure the wire behind the top Square with a Glue Dot. **Tip:** I love making bunches of little cards like this to have handy for spur of the moment card or gift giving. It takes the pressure off and invites in gratitude and fun!

Actual Size: 2" wide x 2" high

BASKET OF LOVE
THANK YOU NOTE

SUPPLY LIST: Sizzix® Dies Large Basket, Large Hearts **Paper** Little Sizzles™ Paper Pad "Pastels" by Sizzix™, Color Wheel™ Bitty Scrap Pad "Hydrangea" and "Flamingo Pink" by Provo Craft®, Nutmeg Cardstock **Miscellaneous** Clear Alphabitties™ "Parlor White" by Provo Craft®, Scissors, Pink Wired Ribbon, Black Micron Pen .03 by Sakura, Pink Writer Pen by Zig, Xyron Adhesive, Glue Pen by Zig

Tip: Try making a few of the Hearts with the darker Flamingo Pink paper for contrast. **Tip:** If you tie the ribbon around the handle of only the front Basket, the recipient doesn't have to untie it to open the card. **Tip:** It's fun to add one or two little Hearts that are tucked into the back Basket with personal messages on the backs OR inside the fold. A simple "pull" tag can be adhered to the back of the "message hearts" so that they can be appreciated.

Alternative Sayings:
"All of My Love for You"
"Bunches of Love"
"I'll Never Run out of Love for You"

Actual Size: 3-3/8" wide x 4-1/2" high

Actual Size: 4-1/8" wide x 4-1/2" high

a heartfelt thanks

gracias   merci

grazie   a lot

GRACIAS HEART
CARD

SUPPLY LIST: Sizzix®Dies Medium Hearts Primitive, Large Squares **Paper** Color Wheel™ Cardstock Scrap Pad "Crayon Box Palette" by Provo Craft®, Color Wheel™ Scrap Pad "Sunflower" by Provo Craft®, Bitty Scrap Pad "All Stars" by Provo Craft®, Shiny White Glitter Paper by Kodak, White Cardstock **Miscellaneous** Coluzzle® Card & Envelope Template, Oval Template, Cutting Mat and Guarded™ Swivel Knife by Provo Craft®; Scissors; Black Micron Pen .03 by Sakura; Xyron Adhesive

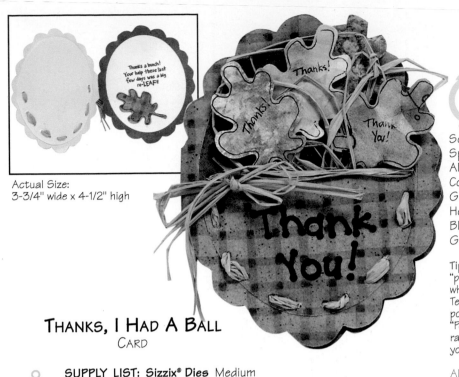

Actual Size:
3-3/4" wide x 4-1/2" high

RE-LEAF
THANK YOU NOTE

SUPPLY LIST: Sizzix® Dies Large Scallop Oval Frame, Small Leaf #1 **Paper** Little Sizzles™ Paper Pad "Pastels" by Sizzix™, Bitty Scrap Pad "French Country" by Provo Craft®, Soft Watercolor Scrap Pad "Autumn Splendor" by Provo Craft® **Miscellaneous** Alphabitties™ "Black Fat Dot" by Provo Craft®; Coluzzle® Oval Template, Cutting Mat, and Guarded® Swivel Knife by Provo Craft®; Tiny Hole Punch by Provo Craft®; Raffia; Scissors; Black Micron Pen .03 & .08 by Sakura; Zig Glue Pen; Xyron Adhesive

Tip: Trim the Oval cut out in half to form your "pocket" to hold the raffia and Leaves. Cut the white cardstock backing (with the Coluzzle® Oval Template), a little larger than the cut out Oval portion of your Frame. This will secure the front "Pocket" onto the front of the card. Lace with raffia. **Tip:** Save a few remaining Leaves to decorate your envelope.

Alternative Sayings:
"Be Leaf it or not, I Love You!"
"Happy Autumn'versary"
"I Can't Be Leaf . . . (insert any exclamation here)"
"What a Re-Leaf it is to always know you're there!"

THANKS, I HAD A BALL
CARD

SUPPLY LIST: Sizzix® Dies Medium Grass, Small Soccer Ball **Paper** Little Sizzles™ Paper Pad "Pastels" and "Rainbow" by Sizzix™ **Miscellaneous** Alphabitties™ "Fat Dot Green" and "Fat Dot Black" by Provo Craft®, Scissors, Black Writer Pen by Zig, Xyron Adhesive

Tip: Trim the Grass so that you have a "tuft" to adhere in front of the Ball. Adhere the rest of the Grass on the front of the inside of the Ball.

Alternative Use:
Use this as a thank you note to your soccer coach!

Actual Size: 2-7/8" wide x 1-3/4" high

MOOO-CHAS GRACIAS
CARD

SUPPLY LIST: Sizzix® Dies Large Cow, Medium Cowboy Hat **Paper** Little Sizzles™ Paper Pad "Watercolors" and "Pastels" by Sizzix™, Fibers by Scrappin' Essentials, White Cardstock, Red Suede Paper **Miscellaneous** Alphabitties™ "Wedge Black" by Provo Craft®, Yellow Raffia, Scissors, Black Micron Pen .03 by Sakura, Xyron Adhesive

Tip: Trim the Cowboy Hat a little thinner on the top to look like a sombrero. **Tip:** Cut one black Cow and one white Cow. Use the black Cow to make the spots and hooves.

Alternative Saying:
"Sorry To Hear that you're Moooving!"

Actual Size:
5-1/4" wide x 5" high

Chapter Ten

SPECIAL OCCASIONS

SPECIAL OCCASIONS

We've all wandered down the aisles, scanning listlessly the rows after rows of cards, looking for the perfect one to express just how we feel. Usually we walk away disappointed or we compromise and say, "This will do". Now we can make the perfect card every time: the perfect Mother's Day card for the mom who's into her Harley; or the Christmas card for your friends in the Bahamas. Now you'll have just the right thing for even the most unique person on your list.

Actual Size: 3-1/4" wide x 4-1/2" high

HAPPY EASTER BUNNY
CARD

SUPPLY LIST: Sizzix® Die Small Eggs **Paper** Little Sizzles™ Paper Pad "Pastels" and "Watercolors" by Sizzix™, Color Wheel™ Scrap Pad "Hydrangea" by Provo Craft® **Miscellaneous** Scissors, Black Micron Pen .03 by Sakura, Xyron Adhesive

Tip: Cut two of the white Egg shapes. Fold one in half vertically and trim out two crescent shaped "ears" to adhere in back of your bunny's body. Hand cut the triangle nose and ear insides. **Tip:** Cut the thin black cardstock strips with a paper trimmer. *See Basket instructions on page 72 (Basket of Love).

Alternative Sayings:
"Hoppy Easter"
"Hippity Hoppity, Easter's On It's Way"

MERRY CHRISTMAS
SNOWFLAKE NOTE

SUPPLY LIST: Sizzix® Dies Large Square #2, Snowflake **Paper** Bitty Gone Big™ "Lavender Sachet" by Provo Craft®, Bitty™ Scrap Pad "Dots, Speckles & Squiggles" by Provo Craft®, Color Wheel™ Scrap Pad "Hydrangea" by Provo Craft® **Miscellaneous** Black Pen, Silver Eyelet

Tip: This can also be used as a To/From tag.

Alternative Saying:
"Welcome Winter"

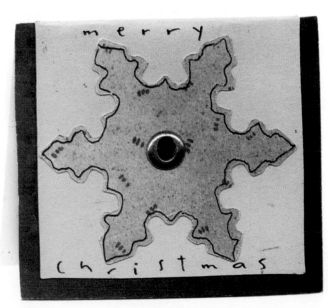

Actual Size: 2-1/4" wide x 2" high (folded)

SUPER STAR TEACHER
CARD

SUPPLY LIST: Sizzix® Dies Fun Serif Alphabet, Large Stars **Paper** Bitty™ Scrap Pad "All Stars" and Color Wheel™ "Apple Red", "Ocean Blue", "Sunflower" and Leaf Green" by Provo Craft®; Glitter Paper **Miscellaneous** Xyron Adhesive

Tip: Put glitter paper behind letters so they really 'pop' out at you. When you die-cut the Sizzix® letters, alternate the colors. You may want to back the card behind the glitter paper to make the inside look nice and neat.

Alternative Sayings:
Instead of "Teacher" use any name or "You're A Super Star"

Actual Size: 6-5/8" wide x 5" high

Actual Size: 3" wide x 4-1/2" high

COOKIES
CARD

SUPPLY LIST: Sizzix® Die Large Jar & Label **Paper** Little Sizzles™ Paper Pad "Classics", "Earth Tones" and "Pastels" by Sizzix™, Color Wheel™ Scrap Pad "Apple Red" by Provo Craft®, Vellum **Miscellaneous** Font: "PC Childish" Never A Dull Moment PC HugWare™ CD by Provo Craft®, Alphabitties™ "Kid's Black" by Provo Craft®, Chalk by Craf-T Products, Twine, Scissors, Xyron Adhesive

Tip: To make the cookies, try using the Large Circles die and trimming with scissors here and there. **Tip:** What a fun way to share a favorite recipe with those that you love. Feel free to change the colors to match the season of your gift or the flavor of your recipe.

Alternative Sayings:
"In the Cookie of Life, You're the Chocolate Chips"
"From the Kitchen of..."

Actual Size: 3" wide x 3-1/2" high

HAPPY LOVE DAY
CARD

SUPPLY LIST: Sizzix® Dies Large Rectangle #1, Medium Hearts Primitive **Paper** Color Wheel™ Scrap Pad "Apple Red" by Provo Craft®, White Vellum **Miscellaneous** Font: "PC Stone Script" Little Images and "PC Block Italic" For Font Sakes PC HugWare™ CD by Provo Craft®, Silver Eyelets by Doodlebug, Eyelet Setting Tool, Hammer by Simple Ideas, Scissors, Xyron Adhesive

Tip: Fold all of your red patterned papers in half and die-cut them individually. Make sure that you leave an edge where the fold is. Layer them alongside the left edge of the card and glue them all down. Remember to keep them overlapping. **Tip:** Valentines Day is the perfect time to spread a little love around. When a card is as quick and easy to make as this one, you can spread around a LOT!

Alternative Saying:
"I Love You with All My Hearts"

LOVE LETTER
CARD

SUPPLY LIST: Sizzix® Dies Medium Hearts Primitive, Large Rectangle #1, Large Square #2 **Paper** Little Sizzles™ Paper Pad "Watercolors" by Sizzix™, Pathways™ ScrapPad "Romance" by Provo Craft®, Vellum **Miscellaneous** Fibers by Scrappin' Essentials, Art Accentz™ "Clear Beads" by Provo Craft®, Page Protector by C-Thru, Chalk by Craf-T Products, Key Charm, Glue Pen by Zig, Art Accentz™ "Terrifically Tacky Tape™ Sheets" by Provo Craft®, Xyron Adhesive, Brown Writer by Zig

Tip: Xyron the floral paper to the speckled paper, then cut with the Rectangle #1 die. Position half of the card under the large Square #2 die to make the window inside. **Tip:** To make any Sizzix® die sparkle, just die-cut of your desired paper, then die-cut the same shape out of Terrifically Tacky Sheets. Apply on top of the paper shape. Remove top adhesive backing, and dip into clear beads!

Alternative Use:
This would make a super anniversary card, or a card welcoming a new baby.

Actual Size: 4-3/8" wide x 3-3/8" high

BE MINE
GARLAND

SUPPLY LIST Sizzix® Dies: Medium Hearts Primitive **Paper** Color Wheel™ Scrap Pad "Black Cherry" by Provo Craft® **Miscellaneous** Alphabet Stamps by Hero Arts, Black Ink Pad by Close To My Heart, Burgundy Raffia, Rectangle Hole Punch

Tip: Accordion fold two and die-cut separate sections of Primitive Hearts, then connect them together in the center with raffia.**Tip:** Lace the raffia through the hole punches to make this card into a garland. Remember not to fold more than three layers.

Alternative Sayings:
"I Love You"
"Be Mine"
"Will You Marry Me?"
" I Do"

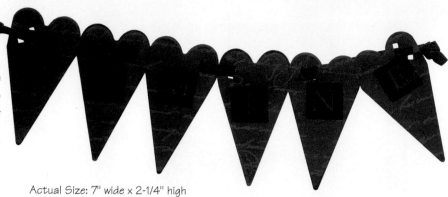

Actual Size: 7" wide x 2-1/4" high

WISHING YOU A
HAPPY ST. PATRICK'S DAY
CARD

SUPPLY LIST: Sizzix® Dies Large Hearts; Medium Leaf, Stem **Paper** Little Sizzles™ Paper Pad "Pastels" by Sizzix™, Color Wheel™ Cardstock Scrap Pad "Tropical" by Provo Craft®, Bitty Scrap Pad "Sunflower Yellow" and "Calypso Green" by Provo Craft® **Miscellaneous** Font: "Block Italic" For Font Sakes PC HugWare™ CD by Provo Craft®, Scissors, Adhesive Tabs by Pioneer

Tip: Use the hearts from the Hearts die to create your own shamrocks. Fold all the Hearts down the center to create a "vein" in the shamrock leaves. **Tip:** When placing the completed shamrock shapes on the card, hang a few off the edge to make a more natural random pattern.

Alternative Sayings:
"Happy St. Paddy's Day"
"Luck of the Irish to You"
"Good Luck be with You"

Actual Size: 5-3/4" wide x 8-3/4" high

SPRING
TAG

SUPPLY LIST Sizzix® Dies: Large Tags, Small Leaf #1 Tiny **Paper** Little Sizzles™ "Earth Tones" by Sizzix™, Color Wheel™ Cardstock "Pineneedle" by Provo Craft® **Miscellaneous** Pathways™ "Heartland Green" Alphabitties™ by Provo Craft®, Plastic Dragonfly Accent, Raffia, Eyelets, Magic Mesh by Avant Card, Small Circle Punch, Page Protector by C-Thru

Tip: Cut two clear squares of clear page protector and place the Leaf in between the plastic pieces. Place this between the leaf patterned paper that has been 'cut on the fold' with the Tag. Sew or glue the two folded pieces together to secure your window.

Actual Size:
2" wide x
4-1/8" high

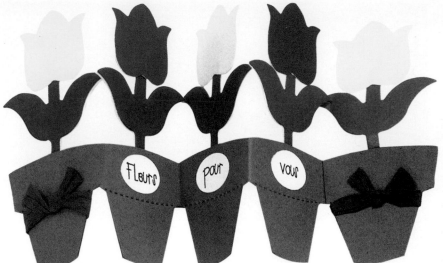

FLEURS POUR VOUS
CARD

SUPPLY LIST Sizzix® Dies: Medium Plant Pots, Medium Tulip **Paper** Little Sizzles™ Paper Pad "Pastels" and "Classics" by Sizzix™, Color Wheel™ Cardstock Scrap Pad "Crayon Box Palette" by Provo Craft®, White Cardstock **Miscellaneous** "Large Oval" Punch by Family Treasures, Red Raffia, Scissors, Black Micron Pen .03 by Sakura, Xyron Adhesive

Tip: Accordion fold and die-cut two sections of pots and connect at the center with adhesive. Slip tulips inbetween front and back of plant pots.

Alternative Saying:
"I Love You"
"Happy Easter"

Actual Size: 1-7/8" wide x 3-3/4" high (folded) (8" unfolded)

EASTER BUNNY
CARD

SUPPLY LIST: Sizzix® Die Small Eggs **Paper** Little Sizzles™ Paper Pad "Pastels" and "Watercolors" by Sizzix™, **Miscellaneous** Micron Pen .03 by Sakura, Glue Pen by Zig

Tip: Cut the bunny ears from the sides of the Egg.

Alternative Saying:
"Hoppy" Easter

Actual Size: 1-1/8" wide x 2-3/8" high

Actual Size:
1-1/2" wide x 3" high

EASTER
TAG CARD

SUPPLY LIST: Sizzix® Dies Large Tags, Small Eggs **Paper** Bitty Scrap Pad "French Country" and "Just Ducky Baby" by Provo Craft® **Miscellaneous** Light Yellow and Light Lavender Raffia, Scissors, Black Micron Pen .03 by Sakura, Glue Dots, Xyron Adhesive

Tip: Wrap the raffia "bows" around each Egg and nestle them into the grass. Draw thin lines around the Eggs with a fine black pen to pop them out from the background Tag. Tie this Tag with raffia or ribbon to your child's Easter basket or onto a pot of forced bulbs given to a friendly neighbor. **Tip:** This Tag also works well for an Easter Brunch or Easter Dinner place card. Just write the name of each guest on the bottom or inside of the Tag.

HAPPY MOTHER'S DAY
CARD

SUPPLY LIST: Sizzix® Dies Large Rectangle #1, Large Squares, Medium Stars Primitive **Paper** Color Wheel™ Cardstock Scrap Pad "Sherbet" by Provo Craft®; Bitty™ Scrap Pad "French Country", "Fabric Textures", "Dots, Squiggles and Speckles" by Provo Craft®; Vellum **Miscellaneous** Clear Alphabitties™ "Pixie Serif Black" by Provo Craft®, Tiny Tag by Avery, Small Hole Punch by Provo Craft®, Small Brads, Green Sheer Ribbon, Scissors, Black Micron Pen .03 by Sakura, Pop Dots by All Night Media, Xyron Adhesive

Tip: Trim vellum a little smaller than your Rectangle. Line them up together (centering the Vellum), and punch the holes at the same time. **Tip:** Trim a few of the Squares down to fit on the Rectangle.

Alternative Sayings:
"You are my Shining Star"
"When You Wish Upon a Star . . . "

Actual Size: 4" wide x 3-1/4" high

HAPPY FATHER'S DAY
CARD

SUPPLY LIST: Sizzix® Die Large Tags **Paper** Little Sizzles™ Paper Pad "Earth Tones" by Sizzix™, Scrap Pad "Fish All Day" by Provo Craft® **Miscellaneous** Font: "PC Lorisans" Fontmania PC HugWare™ CD by Provo Craft®, Fibers by On The Fringe, 1/8" Hole Punch (w/handle), Light Box, Scissors, Black Micron Pen .03 by Sakura, Xyron Adhesive, Easy-Stick Tape Runner by Manco, Inc.

Tip: Use an 1/8" hole punch to punch out the edges of the fish "stamps" instead of scissors, to create that perfect stamp pattern. **Tip:** To get the greeting exactly where you'd like it, just print it out with the font of your choice on plain computer paper. Now use a light box and black pen to trace the greeting in the perfect place!

Alternative Sayings:
"You're a Great Catch"
"So Glad I Caught You"

Actual Size: 1-3/4" wide X 3-3/4" high (folded)

78

CRACKED EASTER EGG
CARD

SUPPLY LIST Sizzix® Dies: Large Egg Cracked, Small Eggs, Small Bird **Paper** Bitty™ Scrap Pad "Tropical Colors" by Provo Craft®, White Cardstock **Miscellaneous** Yellow and Orange Felt, Black Beads for Eyes, Easter Grass

Tip: After die-cutting the Cracked Egg from white cardstock, cut the edge with decorative scissors. Tuck the easter grass under the Eggs a little before gluing down.

Actual Size: 7" wide x 5" high

FOR MOM
CARD

SUPPLY LIST: Sizzix® Die Small Dragonfly **Paper** Little Sizzles™ Paper Pad "Watercolors" and "Pastels" by Sizzix™, Bitty Color Wheel™ Paper Pad "Black Cherry" by Provo Craft® **Miscellaneous** Clear Alphabitties™ "Wrought Iron Gold" by Provo Craft®; Coluzzle® Card & Envelope Template, Cutting Mat, and Guarded™ Swivel Knife by Provo Craft®; Brass Wire by Artistic Wire, Wire Cutting Tool, Wire Pliers, Tiny Hole Punch, Scissors, Xyron Adhesive

Tip: Punch two tiny holes in the Dragonfly's head. Thread the wire through the holes and up through the top of the window of the card. Curl the tops of the wire after they go through the window and Dragonfly's head. **Tip:** Using the Coluzzle® Card & Envelope Template, make three different size cards and coordinating envelopes. It even allows you to make cards with cut out "windows" in the center.

Alternative Sayings:
"Happy Spring!"
"Spring is in the Air"

Actual Size: 5" wide x 7" high

79

HAPPY MOTHER'S DAY
CARD

SUPPLY LIST: Sizzix® Dies Medium Border Ivy, Small Flower #1 (flower petals) **Paper** "Wedding Day" Scrap Pad by Provo Craft®, Color Wheel™ Cardstock Scrap Pad "Sherbet" by Provo Craft® **Miscellaneous** Clear Alphabitties™ "Parlor Sherbet" by Provo Craft®; Coluzzle® Card & Envelope Template, Cutting Mat and Guarded™ Swivel Knife by Provo Craft®; Jewelry Loops; Scissors; Black Micron Pen .03 by Sakura; Xyron Adhesive

Tip: Use the leaves from the Ivy Border to adhere behind the Flowers. To make your Flowers look beautiful from the front and the back, just cut another Flower and adhere it back to back. This will cover up the leaves on the back as well!

Alternative Saying:
"Hang in There!"

Actual Size: 4-1/4" wide x 5-1/2" high

"FORE" MY DAD
FATHER'S DAY CARD

SUPPLY LIST Sizzix® Die Large Pennant **Paper** Little Sizzles™ Paper Pad "Pastels" and "Earth Tones" by Sizzix™, Pathways™ Paper Pad "Grass" by Provo Craft®, Bitty Gone Big™ "Blueberry Pie" by Provo Craft® **Miscellaneous** Clear Alphabitties™ "Pixie Serif" by Provo Craft®, Clear Letters "Pixie Serif" by Provo Craft®, Golf Stickers by Jolee's Boutique, Grey Chalk by Craf-T Products, Tiny Gold Brads, Scissors, Black Micron Pen .03 by Sakura, Xyron Adhesive, Pop Dots by All Night Media

Tip: Cut little 'tufts' of grass from the grass paper to pop out of the field. These add dimension and create shadows that add interest. **Tip:** Use the tiny gold brads to secure the Pennant around the pole. **Tip:** Put "my dad" inside the Pennant using Alphabitty letter stickers.

Alternative Sayings:
"Thanks for helping me through all of those 'rough' times"
"Enjoy your Retirement!"
"All my friends are 'green' with envy that I have you!"

Actual Size: 5-1/4" wide x 5-7/8" high

DAD
CARD

SUPPLY LIST Sizzix® Die: Medium Fern **Paper** Little Sizzles™ Paper Pad "Earth Tones" by Sizzix™, Bitty Scrap Pad "French Country Colors" and "Crackled Antiques/Faux Finishes" by Provo Craft® **Miscellaneous** Coluzzle® Card & Envelope Template, Cutting Mat and Guarded™ Swivel Knife by Provo Craft®; Chalk by Craf-T Products; Tiny Gold Brads by ICL Premier-Grip; Bone Folder; Scissors; Black Micron Pen .02 by Sakura; Xyron Adhesive

Tip: Use brown chalk on the torn edges of this card to give it a rustic, yet artsy feel. Draw a thin line around all of the Ferns. This is the perfect card for anyone who loves the out doors. **Tip:** Lining an envelope with the Coluzzle® Card & Envelope Template is quick and easy. Only cut the top half of the envelope out of the paper that you'd like to line your envelope. Now adhere this to the back side of your paper that you've cut for your envelope, being careful to line it up with the top flap of the envelope. Fold using a bone folder so that your edges are crisp and you've got a perfectly coordinated card and envelope!

Alternative Use:
This would also work well as a Sympathy Card.

Actual Size:
4-1/4" wide x
5-1/2" high

HAPPY 4TH OF JULY
CARD

SUPPLY LIST: Sizzix® Dies Large Squares, Large Firecracker, Medium Stars Primitive **Paper** Color Wheel™ Scrap Pad "Apple Red" and "Blueberry" by Provo Craft®, Crinkled Gold Cardstock, White Embossed Cardstock **Miscellaneous** Clear Alphabitties™ "Wedge Red" by Provo Craft®, Teeny Gold Eyelets by Hyglo, Teeny Gold Eyelet Setting Tool, Blue Chalk by Craf-T Products, Stiff Paintbrush or Make-Up Applicator, White Thread, Hammer by Simple Ideas, Scissors, Black Micron Pen .03 by Sakura, Xyron Adhesive

Tip: You can cut your time by 5 minutes if you connect the banners with Bradletz™ instead of eyelets **Tip:** Chalk with blue chalk when the card is done so that a little bit of blue shows up on the red stripes of the flag and Firecracker. **Tip:** This would be fun to use as an invitation for a Fourth of July BBQ! Just include the information on the back sides of the Squares. **Tip:** Fold this accordion style when placing it in an envelope so that the card unfolds as you lift it out! **Tip:** Trim down the "wick" of the Firecracker so that you can fit more of it onto the Square.

Alternative Invitation Sayings:
"Fourth of July BBQ"
"Come to a neighborhood bike parade"
"Please come and listen to my report on President Lincoln"

Actual Size:
2" wide x 6-1/2" high

HAPPY FOURTH OF JULY
CARD

SUPPLY LIST: Sizzix® Die Large Firecracker **Paper** Little Sizzles™ Paper Pad "Pastels" by Sizzix™, Color Wheel™ Paper Pad "Ocean Blue" by Provo Craft®, Bitty Gone Big™ "Cross Your Heart" and "First Star" by Provo Craft® **Miscellaneous** Clear Alphabitties™ "Parlor Black" by Provo Craft®, White Eyelets by Doodlebug, Eyelet Setting Tool, Hammer by Simple Ideas, White Thread, Needle, Paper Trimmer, Scissors, Black Micron Pen .03 by Sakura, Xyron Adhesive, Zig Glue Pen

Tip: Everyone will get a big bang out of this card! You could also try using it as a name tag for a party or even a sales meeting around the Fourth of July. **Tip:** After cutting your Firecracker, line up the center portions of both pieces with your paper back to back. Now punch holes for your eyelets two at a time. This ensures even eyelets! **Tip:** Double thread your needle. Start from the back and come up through the white cardstock on any side. Tie a pretty big knot so that your thread doesn't come out. Leave yourself about 2 inches of thread to work with at the end of your knot. Stitch the thread around as shown and tie end to your knot in back.

Alternative Sayings:
As a card for your Dad,
   "Pops, You're the Best"
You could attach it to an interesting article and say,
   "I got a bang out of this, give me a call!"
"I Get a bang out of You"

Actual Size:
2-3/8" wide x 5-1/2" high

WELCOME BACK TO SCHOOL
CARD

SUPPLY LIST: Sizzix® Die Large Jelly Frame **Paper** Color Wheel™ Scrap Pad "Sunflower" and "Leaf Green" by Provo Craft® **Miscellaneous** Vellum Sticker "Apple Harvest" by Provo Craft®, Scissors, Black Writer Pen by Zig, Xyron Adhesive

Tip: Fold patterned paper in half and die-cut the Jelly Frame, leaving one side of the card on the fold. Trim a piece of yellow paper to cover the opening in the frame. **Tip:** My children have been so lucky to have great teachers in school. Some of their teachers have even gone the extra mile and sent little cards, notes or letters before school began, welcoming them to their class for the new year. The kids loved receiving those small tokens and looked forward to that first day, and feeling as if they already "knew" their teachers.

Alternative Saying:
"Thanks for a Great Year"

Actual Size: 4-7/8" wide x 3-3/4" high

THANKFUL
TAG

SUPPLY LIST: Sizzix® Dies Small Cornucopia, Small Fruit, Large Tags **Paper** Little Sizzles™ Paper Pad "Watercolors" by Sizzix™, Sage Cardstock by Provo Craft®, Little Sizzles™ Textured Handmade Papers "Leather" by Sizzix™ **Miscellaneous** Pathways™ Alphabitties™ "Sepia" by Provo Craft®, Chalk by Craf-T Products, Wire, Eyelets, Bradletz™ by Provo Craft®, Raffia, Eyelet Setting Tool, Hammer by Simple Ideas

Tip: Be sure to chalk around the edges of the Fruit and the edges of the card before gluing them together. Place little wire curly-Q's in between the Fruit. **Tip:** Use Bradletz™ as grapes.

Actual Size: 2" wide x 3-1/2" high (not including raffia)

Actual Size: 5" wide x 7" high

BE-LEAF IN YOURSELF
CARD

SUPPLY LIST: Sizzix® Die Small Leaf #1 **Paper** Bitty™ Scrap Pad "Happy Halloween" and "Primary Colors" by Provo Craft®, Color Wheel™ "Black Cherry" and "Sunflower" by Provo Craft®, Bitty Gone Big™ "Cross Your Heart" and "First Star" by Provo Craft®, White Cardstock **Miscellaneous** Eyelets by Doodlebug, Chalk by Craf-T Products, Eyelet Setting Tool, Hammer by Simple Ideas, Scissors, Glue Pen by Zig

Tip: When you place the Leaves on the card, be sure to alternate them up and down. Also, chalk the Leaves and edges of the sunflower paper before putting the card together.

83

Actual Size: 5-1/2" wide x 4-1/4" high

BOO
CARD

SUPPLY LIST: Sizzix® Die Large Rectangle #1, Medium Bat, Small Fun Serif Uppercase Letters "B", "O", and "!" **Paper** Bitty Scrap Pad "Mad About Plaid", "Thru The Year" and "Happy Halloween" by Provo Craft® **Miscellaneous** Clear Alphabitties™ "Wedge Black" by Provo Craft®, Chalk by Craf-T Products, Black Wire by Artistic Wire, Black Eyelets by Doodlebug, Eyelet Setting Tool, Hammer by Simple Ideas, Scissors, Paper Trimmer, Black Micron Pen .03 by Sakura, Xyron Adhesive

Tip: Place the eyelets onto Rectangle #1 before adhering it onto the mats behind it. **Tip:** An easy way to make any quick card is by folding an 8-1/2" x 11" piece of white cardstock in half, and just adding the cover of the card to the front of your white cardstock. This allows you to save a bit on decorative paper and makes a darling card as well!

Alternative Sayings:
"Happy Halloween"
"Happy Boo Day"

HAPPY HALLOWEEN
CARD

SUPPLY LIST: Sizzix® Dies Large Circles, Medium Bat **Paper** Little Sizzles™ Paper Pad "Watercolors" and "Pastels" by Sizzix™, Vellum **Miscellaneous** Clear Alphabitties™ "Parlor Black" by Provo Craft®, Gold Raffia, Black Brads, Paper Trimmer, Scissors, Black Micron Pen .03 by Sakura, Xyron Adhesive

Tip: Unwrap your raffia and run it through the Xyron machine adhesive cartridge. Place it onto a piece of white cardstock. Now cut out a circle with the Circles die over the raffia. Adjust Circle over a Circle on the die and cut again to form the moon shape. Line with your black pen. **Tip:** Vellum is a wonderful way to soften dynamic patterns. It's also a super medium to write on with a pen because if you happen to make a little mistake, you can scrape it off with the blade of a craft knife.

Alternative Sayings:
"Boo To You"
"Happy Boo Day"

Actual Size:
5" wide x
3-1/2" high

CANDY CANE
TO: FROM: TAG

SUPPLY LIST: Sizzix® Dies Large Tags, Medium Candy Cane, Medium Bow **Paper** Little Sizzles™ Paper Pad "Classics" by Sizzix™, Bitty Scrap Pad "Ivory Coast" by Provo Craft® **Miscellaneous** Clear Alphabitties™ "Wrought Iron Patina" by Provo Craft®, Scissors, Black Micron Pen .01 & .05 by Sakura, Xyron Adhesive

Tip: It's okay to let some of the die overlap the Tag. Try using any die that you have to make seasonal To/From Tags!

Alternative Sayings:
"You're the Sweetest Thing"
"Thanks for being so Sweet"

Actual Size:
2" wide x 4" high

WIRE MESH
CHRISTMAS TREE
CARD

SUPPLY LIST: Sizzix® Dies Large Scallop Oval Frame, Medium Pine Tree **Paper** Little Sizzles™ Paper Pad "Classics" by Sizzix™ **Miscellaneous** Clear Alphabitties™ "Pixie Serif Gold" by Provo Craft®, Gold Ribbon by Offray, Gold Screen, Gold Snowflake Charms, Gold Thread, Paper Trimmer, Scissors, Black Micron Pen .03 by Sakura, Xyron Adhesive, Glue Dots

Tip: Secure the thread between the two layers of paper that you used to make the front and inside of the card. Use the Glue Dots to secure the snowflake charm to the top of the Tree. **Tip:** Be careful when cutting screen and thin metals with Sizzix®. The edges can be really sharp!

Alternative Use:
Use this card without the snowflake at the top for any winter occasion!

Actual Size: 3-1/4" wide x 4-1/2" high

SNOW FLURRIES
CARD

SUPPLY LIST: Sizzix® Dies Large Squares, Small Snowflake **Paper** Back To Nature "Snow Flurries" by Provo Craft®, White Cardstock **Miscellaneous** Light Blue Acrylic Jewels by Westrim, Paper Trimmer, Black Micron Pen .03 by Sakura, Xyron Adhesive, Glue Dots

Tip: Mat all of your Squares with the snow flurries paper, then mat that section with white cardstock. Adhere the jewels with Glue Dots. **Tip:** Winter can get so dull and dreary in some parts of the country. Why not whip up this fun snowflake card to brighten a snowbound friend's day?

Alternative Sayings:
"Sorry I was a Flake"
"May your Christmas be Merry and Bright"

Actual Size: 7-1/2" high x 5-1/4" wide

CHRISTMAS ORNAMENT
CARD

SUPPLY LIST Sizzix® Dies: Medium Fern, Small Ornament **Paper** Little Sizzles™ Paper Pad "Classics" by Sizzix™, Scrap Pad "Wishes & Dreams" by Provo Craft®, Color Wheel™ Scrap Pad "Avocado" by Provo Craft® **Miscellaneous** Coluzzle® Card & Envelope Template, Cutting Mat and Guarded® Swivel Knife by Provo Craft®; Clear Impressions Stamps "Bitty Christmas Set" by Provo Craft®; Green 30 gauge wire by Artistic Wire; Fresco Ink Pad "Giovanni's Garden" by Stampa Rosa; Tiny Hole Punch by Provo Craft®; Scissors; Stardust Gel Ink Rollerball "Golden-Star" by Sakura; Xyron Adhesive

Tip: Don't be afraid to let shapes hang over the sides of the card. Just turn the card over and trim off the overhanging pieces for a natural scattered look and feel. **Tip:** Create little "hooks" with wire to "hang" your ornaments onto the card's front.

Actual Size: 7" wide x 5" high

CHRISTMAS LIGHTS
CARD

SUPPLY LIST: Sizzix® Die Small Christmas Light **Paper** Little Sizzles™ Paper Pad "Classics" and "Pastels" by Sizzix™; Pathways™ "Pine Boughs" by Provo Craft®; Sparkly Paper in the following colors: Red, Blue, Orange, Green, Yellow, Purple, White, Black; 8-1/2" x 11" cardstock **Miscellaneous** Clear Alphabitties™ "Wedge" by Provo Craft®, Rectangle Punch by Family Treasures, Silver Elastic Cord, Scissors, Xyron Adhesive, Pop Dots by All Night Media

Tip: I love old-fashioned bright, shiny, sparkly lights on a Christmas Tree — the kind we used to have on our tree when I was a child. Each of these Lights can represent your family members, and it's fun to add the four legged members of your family as well! **Tip:** The little flip up Light in the inside of the card could also be used to write "Happy New Year".

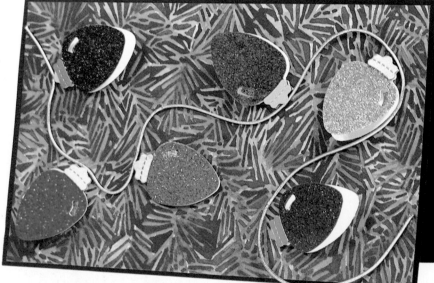

Actual Size: 8-1/2" wide x 5-1/2" high

Alternative Sayings:
"May Your Christmas be Merry & Bright"

HUNG BY THE CHIMNEY WITH CARE
CARD

SUPPLY LIST: Sizzix® Dies Medium Candles, Medium Stocking, Medium Candy Cane, Small Campfire **Paper** Little Sizzles™ Paper Pad "Classics", "Pastels" and "Earth Tones" by Sizzix™, Little Sizzles™ Textured Handmade Papers "Leather" by Sizzix™, Back To Nature "Rock Pathway" by Provo Craft® **Miscellaneous** Alphabitties™ "Pixie Serif Black" by Provo Craft®, Ribbon by Offray, Borders & Corners Stickers "Bordering Branches" by Provo Craft®, Shrink Plastic by Shrinky Dink, Pine Garland Black Micron Pen .02 by Sakura, Brown Writer Pen by Zig, Foam Squares by Peel-n-Stick, Glue Dots, Glue Pen by Zig

Tip: Cut your Candy Canes from shrink plastic, color and bake to make tiny Candy Cane "charms" coming out of the Stockings. Attach with Glue Dots. Tip: Draw "wood grain" with a brown marker on light brown cardstock to make your mantle and logs look realistic.

CHRISTMAS CANDY BASKET
CARD

SUPPLY LIST: Sizzix® Dies Large Basket, Medium Candy Cane, Medium Fern, Small Candy **Paper** Little Sizzles™ Paper Pad "Pastels" and "Rainbow" by Sizzix™, Color Wheel™ Cardstock Scrap Pad "Nature Palette" by Provo Craft®, Bitty Scrap Pad "It's Christmas" by Provo Craft®, Nutmeg Cardstock **Miscellaneous** Scissors, Black Micron Pen .03 by Sakura, Xyron Adhesive

Actual Size: 4-1/4" wide x 1-3/4" high

Tip: Think of all the other shapes you could place into this Basket! Holly and Berries for Christmas, Teddy Bears for a Baby Shower or Baby Gift Card, Apples for a Teacher Card, Pumpkins or Leaves for Fall, Chicks or Bunnies for Easter, Candles for Birthdays . . . the list goes on forever! Tip: Use the inside basket portion to secure all of your goodies into the Basket from the back.

Alternative Sayings:
"Sweets for the Sweet"
"May Your Holidays be filled with Sweetness

SANTA
CARD OR ORNAMENT

SUPPLY LIST: Sizzix® Die Large Santa Head **Paper** Little Sizzles™ Paper Pad "Watercolors" by Sizzix™ **Miscellaneous** Clear Alphabitties™ "Wedge" by Provo Craft®, Various Fabrics, Fusible Bonding, Googly Eyes, Black Micron Pen .03 by Sakura, Xyron Adhesive

Tip: Iron the fusible bonding onto the fabric. Die-cut each piece with the Santa Head. Use the perforation lines to guide you to cut each piece. Tip: Line with folded black cardstock.

Actual Size: 4-1/8" wide x 4-1/2" high

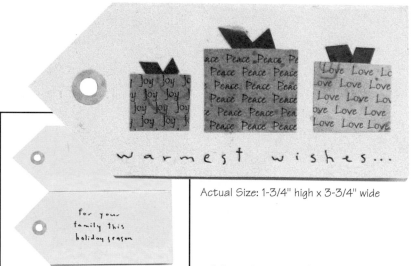

SPARKLY SNOWFLAKES
TAG

SUPPLY LIST: Sizzix® Die Small Snowflake **Paper** Little Sizzles™ Paper Pad "Rainbow" by Sizzix™, Color Wheel™ Scrap Pad "Blueberry" and "Brickyard" by Provo Craft® **Miscellaneous** Alphabitties™ (lowercase) "Blueberry Block" by Provo Craft®, Art Accentz™ "Terrifically Tacky Tape™ Sheets" by Provo Craft®, Shaved Ice Fibers, Eyelet, Eyelet Setting Tool, Hammer by Simple Ideas, Hole Punch, Scissors, Brown Micron Pen .03 by Sakura, Xyron Adhesive

Tip: Cut two of the Snowflakes on the fold so that the recipient enjoys the added excitement of opening each little mini Snowflake "card". **Tip:** To apply Shaved Ice, use Terrifically Tacy Tape™ Sheets to cut out snow flake, then dip in shaved ice.

Alternative Sayings:
You could put "Let" "It' and "Snow" in each Snowflake and send it as a happy card to cheer a friend with the winter doldrums.

Actual Size: 5" wide x 3" high

WARMEST WISHES
TAG CARD

SUPPLY LIST: Sizzix® Dies Large Tags, Large Squares **Paper** Bitty Scrap Pad "Dots, Speckles & Squiggles" by Provo Craft®, Bitty Scrap Pad "Primary Colors" and "French Country" by Provo Craft®, Scrap Pad "Let's Hit the Road" by Provo Craft® **Miscellaneous** PC Sketched (download from internet www.pccrafter.com), Scissors, Xyron Adhesive

Tip: Use your computer to write "love", "joy" and "peace" over and over again on different colors of paper. Die-cut these with your Squares. Some trimming may be necessary to make the presents the size that you'd like. Top with a tiny punched or hand cut bow.

Alternative Sayings:
"These Gifts We Bring"
"To:... From:..."
"The Gifts of the Holidays"

Actual Size: 1-3/4" high x 3-3/4" wide

YOU LIGHT UP MY LIFE
CARD

SUPPLY LIST: Sizzix® Die Small Christmas Light **Paper** Little Sizzles™ Paper Pad "Pastels" and "Classics" by Sizzix™, Vellum **Miscellaneous** Chalks by Craf-T Products, Silver Metallic Embroidery Floss by DMC, Scissors, Small Hole Punch, Black Micron Pen .05 by Sakura, Xyron Adhesive

Tip: Fold white strip of cardstock accordion style two times over, making sure it's approximately 1/8" thinner in size than the widest part of the die shape. Center folds over die and cut. Repeat. Connect both accordions in the center with adhesive. **Tip:** Punch small holes at the tops of light caps and thread silver metallic floss or cording through as shown.

Alternative Saying:
"May your Christmas be Merry and Bright"

Actual Size: 6-1/4" wide x 2" high

HAPPY HOLIDAYS
CARD

SUPPLY LIST: Sizzix® Dies Large Squares, Large Christmas Tree, Medium Stars Primitive **Paper** Little Sizzles™ Paper Pad "Pastels" by Sizzix™, Bitty Gone Big™ "Cross your Heart" and "Lost in the Woods" by Provo Craft®, Gold Shiny Paper by Canford **Miscellaneous** Clear Alphabitties™ "Wrought Iron Gold" by Provo Craft®, "Old Ivy" Paint by Delta, Compressed Sponge by Craf-T Products, Gold Ultra Foil by Reynolds, Tiny Gold Brads, 12" Paper Trimmer, Scissors, Gold Metallic Gel Pen by Tsukineko, Xyron Adhesive, Hermafix Dots

Tip: Die-cut all of your Squares including your Square on the fold. (Make sure that your Square on the fold is facing outward.) Secure them to a sheet of copy paper with your Hermafix Dots. Place them right next to one another, 3 across and 4 down. Now die-cut your Christmas Tree from the compressed sponge material. Hold Tree under running water. Wring out as much water as possible. Dip into your paint, making sure that all of the edges are covered. (I like to do a "test blot" just to make sure.) Center your paint loaded tree sponge over your Squares and place onto Squares. Press evenly over the entire area. Pick up sponge gently, and you'll have a beautiful mosaic! Let these Squares dry completely. When Squares are dry, remove them from the copy paper and place them on the Cross Your Heart paper, about 1/8" apart. Secure with a permanent adhesive. Add decorative lining and an Alphabitty title. Place the brads randomly on the Tree to look like ornaments. Write a personal sentiment in the only folded Square. Place the Star, die-cut from the Reynolds Foil, atop the Tree.

Alternative Saying:
"Merry Christmas"

Actual Size:
6-1/2" wide x
8" high

MERRY CHRISTMAS
Card

SUPPLY LIST: Sizzix® Dies Large Doll Body, Large Doll Girl Hair #1, Large Doll Boy Hair #1, Large Doll Overalls, Large Doll Dresses, Large Doll Winter Clothes, Large Tree Pine, Medium Stars Primitive, Medium Doll Bath Clothes, Small Bitty Body, Small Girl Hair #1, Small Boy Hair #1, Small Shorts & Top, Small Overalls, Small Bitty Swimsuit, Small Bitty Dresses, Small Bitty Pajamas & Bear, Small Doll Shoes #1 **Paper** Little Sizzles™ Paper Pad "Pastels" and "Watercolors" by Sizzix™, Scrap Pad "Winter Holidays" by Provo Craft® **Miscellaneous** Alphabitties™ "Kid's Black" by Provo Craft®, Black Seed Beads by Westrim Crafts, Black Thread by Coats & Clark, Crystal Stickers by Mark Richards Enterprises, Inc., Tiny Buttons by Favorite Findings, Clear Impressions Acrylic Rubber Stamp Faces by Provo Craft®, Black Ink Pad by Delafield Stamp Co., Scissors, Black Micron Pen .03 by Sakura, Hermafix Transfer Dots, Pop Dots by All Night Media

Tip: This card is definitely a family affair! Bring the entire family in to create this keepsake card. Each member can create a doll representing themselves, all dressed up in their Christmas pj's, for your next Christmas greeting card. Change the heights of each Doll by adding and deleting lengths of arms and legs. **Tip:** I highly suggest color copying the original to send out as your Christmas card, then using the original as a title when scrapbooking your Christmas photos.

Alternative Saying:
"From Our Family"

Actual Size: 8-1/8" wide x 6-1/8" high

89

Chapter Eleven

LOOK ALIKE
PAPERDOLLS

LOOK ALIKE PAPERDOLLS

My family recently made a long distance move from Utah back to our native state of California. While preparing for this move, many of my cherished friends came to my aid with boxes, packing and cleaning materials in hand. They spent hours cleaning and wrapping all of the items that were to be packed. Back in California, as I hurriedly unwrapped each piece of my home and my life, it brought to mind the chatter, hard work and smiling faces of all of those girl friends. I remembered the sound of their voices and it felt like it was my birthday, or Christmas morning as I unwrapped each package. I slowed down, unwrapped more slowly, and felt the love that went into this deed. I realized that my friends had given me the most precious gift—their time and their love. I was touched by their support, and missed them terribly. After all of the things were put away, I wanted them to know how much everything they'd done meant to me. I decided on look-alike cards to express my sincere gratitude. I made a paper doll of me, with my arm around each of them. I wanted each of them to know that I remembered THEIR contribution and kindness. I wanted them to know that I loved and cherished THEM. And just maybe by looking at that card at some later date, they'll get a tiny glimpse of my love for them, and those memories that I hold dear.

SNOWFLAKE BOY
JANUARY

SUPPLY LIST: Sizzix® Dies Large Doll Body, Large Doll Winter Clothes, Large Doll Bath Clothes, Large Doll Girl Hair #1, Small Snowflake **Paper** Little Sizzles™ Paper Pad "Pastels", "Rainbow", "Watercolors" and "Earth Tones" by Sizzix™; Bitty Scrap Pad "Primary Colors" by Provo Craft®; Flesh Cardstock **Miscellaneous** Chalk by Craf-T Products, Crystal Lites by Arnold Grummer, Scissors, Black Micron Pen .03 by Sakura, Art Accentz™ "Shimmerz Glue by Provo Craft®, Liquid Adhesive by Tombow

Tip: Trim the bunny slippers down to make the snow boots.
Tip: Use white cardstock to make the Snowflake. Cover Snowflake with your Shimmerz Glue and sprinkle the Crystal Lites on top. Let this dry thoroughly, then adhere to the front of the Body, with the edges underneath the mittens.

Alternative Sayings:
"You Melt my Heart"
"Sorry I was such a flake"
"There's 'snow' way I can express how much I Love You"

Actual Size:
2-3/4" wide x 4-1/4" high
(measurement includes accessories)

VALENTINE GIRL
FEBRUARY

SUPPLY LIST: Sizzix® Dies Large Doll Body, Large Doll Dresses, Large Doll Girl Hair #1, Medium Border Heart **Paper** Little Sizzles™ Paper Pad "Pastels" and "Earth Tones" by Sizzix™; Bitty Gone Big™ "Pink Lady", "Sweetheart Speckles" and "Country Sky" by Provo Craft®; Flesh Cardstock **Miscellaneous** Chalk by Stampin' Up, Tiny Circle Punch by Provo Craft®, Scissors, Black Micron Pen .02 by Sakura, Glue Pen by Zig

Tip: Use a tiny circle punch to make little necklaces and bracelets. **Tip:** Hand cut the garland "rope" that holds the Hearts. Cut out the individual hearts from the Heart border. Cut the rope in little pieces and attach each piece to each Heart so that it looks as if they're going through the rope.

Alternative Sayings:
"I Love You"
"Happy Valentine's Day"
"You Hold my Heart in Your Hands"

Actual Size:
2-7/8" wide x 3-3/4" high
(measurement includes accessories)

91

KITE
MARCH

SUPPLY LIST: Sizzix® Dies Large Squares, Small Bitty Body, Small Bitty Shorts & Top, Small Bitty Overalls **Paper** Little Sizzles™ Paper Pad "Pastels" by Sizzix™, Bitty Scrap Pad "Acapulco Purple" and "Tropical Sun" by Provo Craft® **Miscellaneous** Chalk by Craf-T Products, Wire by Artistic Wire, Wire Cutters, Pliers, Scissors, Black Micron Pen .01 by Sakura, Glue Pen by Zig

Tip: Here's an easy card for a blustery March day. **Tip:** If you'd like to make your doll look up or down, simply snip off the nose or ear and angle the hair.

Actual Size:
3-1/2" wide x
5-7/8" high (including kite)

EASTER BUNNY BOY
APRIL

SUPPLY LIST: Sizzix® Dies Large Doll Body, Large Girl Hair #1, Large Doll Winter Clothes, Medium Doll Bath Clothes **Paper** Little Sizzles™ Paper Pad "Earth Tones" by Sizzix™, Bitty Scrap Pad "Nature Works" by Provo Craft®, Scrap Pad "That's My Baby" by Provo Craft®, White Fuzzy Paper by Wintech, Flesh Cardstock **Miscellaneous** Chalk by Craf-T Products, Tiny Buttons by Blumenthal Lansing Co., Scissors, Black Micron Pen .02 by Sakura, Bond 527 Multi-Purpose Cement, Liquid Adhesive by Tombow

Tip: Use the Girl Hair to trim into a boy's hair style. Hand cut the bunny ears out of your white fuzzy paper. **Tip:** Use the snowsuit hat to make the basket. Now cut an additional basket, and trim around the bottom to make a basket handle. Crinkle the green paper and cut into thin strips to make the grass. Adhere both handle and grass from behind the basket. **Tip:** Chalk lightly with light blue around the bunny outfit and light pink on his cheeks and inside of ears.

Alternative Sayings:
"You're some bunny special"
"Hippity Hoppity, Easter's on its way!"
"Some bunny told me it's your Birthday!"

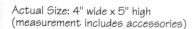

Actual Size: 4" wide x 5" high
(measurement includes accessories)

EASTER GIRL
APRIL

SUPPLY LIST: Sizzix® Dies Large Doll Body, Large Girl Hair #1, Large Doll Overalls, Small Eggs **Paper** Little Sizzles™ Paper Pad "Earth Tones" by Sizzix™; Bitty Scrap Pad "Just Ducky Baby", "Primary Colors" and "Tropical" by Provo Craft®; Flesh Cardstock **Miscellaneous** Chalk by Stampin' Up, Scissors, Black Micron Pen .02 by Sakura, Xyron Adhesive

Tip: Try putting tiny brads or buttons on the girl's overall dress to add dimension. **Tip:** This can also be used as a place card or invitation for a special Easter celebration.

Alternative Sayings:
"You're Eggstra Special"
"Come to our Egg Coloring Party!"
"You're Eggstraordinary!"

Actual Size: 2-7/8" wide x
3-3/4" high
(measurement includes accessories)

Actual Size: 2-7/8" wide x
3-3/4" high
(measurement includes accessories)

MOM-TO-BE
MAY

SUPPLY LIST: Sizzix® Dies Large Doll Body, Large Doll Girl Hair #1, Small Doll Shoes #1 **Paper** Little Sizzles™ Paper Pad "Country" by Sizzix™, Bitty Scrap Pad "French Country" by Provo Craft®, Scrap Pad "Let's Hit the Road" by Provo Craft®, Vellum **Miscellaneous** Chalk by Stampin' Up, Tiny Hole Punch by Provo Craft®, Scissors, Black Micron Pen .02 by Sakura, Glue Pen by Zig

Tip: Here's a simple way to make custom clothes for this (or any) paper doll: After cutting the arms and one leg off, just place a piece of vellum over the body shape and trace where you'd like the clothes to be. Now use this piece of vellum as a template for clothing! Trim the shoes down to match the shoes of your recipient. **Tip:** This card makes a super baby announcement or Mother's Day card, as well as a baby shower gift tag.

Alternative Sayings:
"Congratulations!"
"Happy Mother's Day!"

Actual Size: 2-1-2" wide x 3-3/4" high
(measurement includes accessories)

SWIMSUIT GIRL
JUNE

SUPPLY LIST: Sizzix® Dies Large Doll Body, Large Girl Hair #1, Medium Doll Summer Clothes **Paper** Bitty Scrap Pad "Primary Colors" and "French Country" by Provo Craft®, Green Vellum, Flesh Cardstock **Miscellaneous** Chalk by Stampin' Up, Small Hole Punch by Provo Craft®, Paper Shaper Scissors "Mini Scallop" or "Zig Zag" by Provo Craft®, Scissors, Black Micron Pen .03 by Sakura, Xyron Adhesive

Tip: Use the small hole punch to punch two holes into your green paper. Hand cut the sunglasses around these two holes. Place green vellum behind the "lens". Try placing them over the eyes to look like goggles for a swim party invitation! **Tip:** Trim the bottom of the Girl's Hair to look fringy. **Tip:** Use Scallop or Zig Zag Paper Shaper Scissors to create the ridged cushioned bottoms of the sandals.

Alternative Sayings:
"Come to our BBQ!"
"Happy Fourth of July – from our house to yours"
"It's a 4th of July Block Party at the Tanner's"

COUPLE
JULY

SUPPLY LIST: Sizzix® Dies Large Doll Body, Large Doll Boy Hair #1, Large Doll Girl Hair #1, Large Doll Overalls, Large Doll Winter Clothes, Large Circles, Medium Doll Summer Clothes, Medium Doll Summer Accessories, Medium Stars Primitive, Small Doll Shoes #1 **Paper** Little Sizzles™ Paper Pad "Pastels", "Rainbow", "Watercolors" and "Earth Tones" by Sizzix™; Bitty Gone Big™ "Cross Your Heart", "Country Sky" and "Dots, Squiggles & Speckles" by Provo Craft® **Miscellaneous** Pathways™ Vellum Sticker "Life in America" by Provo Craft®, Chalk by Craf-T Products, Flower Eyelets by Doodlebug, Eyelet Setting Tool, Hammer by Simple Ideas, Scissors, Black Micron Pen .02 by Sakura, Glue Pen by Zig

Tip: Here's a fun idea for an invitation to a 4th of July celebration, summer BBQ or picnic! Sit down with your family and have everyone make a look alike doll of themself. Attach them all together to make a truly memorable keepsake! This might even be a neat way to spend each New Years Eve, and watch your family's view of themself change over the years! **Tip:** Trim down the winter snow beanie to make the baseball cap. **Tip:** Trim the Overalls legs off to make an overall dress. Round the edges of the straps to create a more feminine look. **Tip:** Attach the vellum sticker flag to white cardstock to make it a little more sturdy. It's also a good idea to double the cardstock "pole" that the flag is attached to. **Tip:** Use the 2nd to largest Circle to create the little BBQ.

Alternative Sayings:
"Happy Fourth of July – from our house to yours"
"Come to our BBQ!"
"It's a 4th of July Block Party at the Tanner's"

Actual Size:
4-1/2" wide x 4" high
(measurement includes accessories)

SWIMMING POOL
AUGUST

SUPPLY LIST: Sizzix® Dies Large Doll Body, Large Doll Girl Hair #1, Medium Pool, Medium Doll Summer Accessories, Picket Fence, Medium Grass **Paper** Little Sizzles™ Paper Pad "Pastels" and "Watercolors" by Sizzix™; Bitty Gone Big™ "Under the Haystack", "Country Sky", "Lost in the Woods", "It's Raining, It's Pouring" and "In the Meadow" by Provo Craft®; Flesh Cardstock **Miscellaneous** Pathways™ Clear Alphabitties™ "Traditional Black" by Provo Craft®, Chalk by Craf-T Products, Scissors, Black Micron Pen .03 by Sakura, Glue Pen by Zig

Tip: Use a craft knife to cut a slit in the water to put the legs through. Hand cut little flippers if desired. Next, cut a curved "V" shaped slit into the hair as shown. Insert the head into the Hair and adhere. **Tip:** Cut a tiny flower out of "In the Meadow" paper to attach to the sand bucket.

Alternative Sayings:
"Bon Voyage",
"You've Been Working Too Hard – Come over and RELAX!"
"You're Invited to a Swim Party"
"I Sink I Love You"
"I'm Sinking of You"

Actual Size: 6" wide x 3-1/2" high
(measurement includes accessories)

TEACHER
SEPTEMBER

SUPPLY LIST: Sizzix® Dies Large Doll Body, Large Doll Girl Hair #1, Large Doll Dresses, Large Doll Overalls **Paper** Little Sizzles™ Paper Pad "Pastels" and "Earth Tones" by Sizzix™, Bitty™ Scrap Pad "French Country" and "Primary Colors" by Provo Craft®, Flesh Cardstock **Miscellaneous** Chalk by Stampin' Up, Scissors, Black Micron Pen .02 by Sakura, Xyron Adhesive

Tip: What teacher wouldn't love your child's rendition of him or her made into this little card? It'd also be a wonderful keepsake for the bus driver who rarely gets thanked for his or her services. **Tip:** By lining the shirt with a fine black pen, you can make it into a collared shirt! Place tiny brads or circular buttons on the front. **Tip:** By trimming the Hair and the Shoes, you can make custom outfits to match anyone's style!

Alternative Sayings:
"For an A Plus Teacher"
"You're the Apple of my Eye!"
"Thanks for taking us to the Planetarium!"

Actual Size: 2-7/8" wide x 3-3/4" high
(measurement includes accessories)

COWBOY COSTUME
OCTOBER

SUPPLY LIST: Sizzix® Dies Large Doll Body, Large Doll Boy Hair #1, Medium Doll Bedtime Bear, Medium Cowboy Accessories **Paper** Little Sizzles™ Paper Pad "Pastels", "Watercolors", "Earth Tones" and "Country" by Sizzix™; Bitty Gone Big™ "Country Sky" by Provo Craft® **Miscellaneous** Ultra Foil by Reynolds, Chalk by Craf-T Products, Rectangle Punch by Provo Craft®, Scissors, Black Micron Pen .03 by Sakura, Brown Writer by Zig, Glue Pen by Zig

Tip: Trim down the Pajamas for the pants and the shirt. Cut a "V" at the neck and draw in the collar and cuff details. **Tip:** Punch a rectangle through the foil. Now trim around that rectangle to make the belt buckle.

Alternative Sayings:
"Howdy Partner!"
"Please come to my Cowboy Party"
"Thanks – We had a Rootin' Tootin' Good Time!"

Actual Size: 3" wide x 4" high
(measurement includes accessories)

GIVING THANKS PUMPKIN BOY
NOVEMBER

SUPPLY LIST: Sizzix® Dies Large Doll Body, Large Doll Boy Hair #1, Large Doll Overalls, Small Doll Shoes #1, Small Pumpkin **Paper** Little Sizzles™ Paper Pad "Pastels" and "Earth Tones" by Sizzix™, Bitty Gone Big™ "Pumpkin Goop" by Provo Craft®, Bitty Scrap Pad "And Summer Too" by Provo Craft®, Scrap Pad "Awesome Athletes" and "Country Fall" by Provo Craft® **Miscellaneous** Chalk by Stampin' Up, Thin Twine, Scissors, Black Micron Pen .03 by Sakura, Xyron Adhesive

Tip: Make a tiny little tag from white cardstock that says "Giving Thanks". Place around the Pumpkin's stem with thin twine. **Tip:** Round off the hand at the wrist with your scissors and place on top of the Pumpkin. If you'd like, you can draw a Jack-o-Lantern face onto the Pumpkin.

Alternative Sayings:
"Happy Thanksgiving"
"I'm Thankful for You"
"Happy Halloween"

Actual Size: 2-7/8" wide x 3-3/4" high
(measurement includes accessories)

LITTLE BOY WITH TEDDY BEAR
DECEMBER

SUPPLY LIST: Sizzix® Dies Large Doll Body, Large Doll Boy Hair #1, Medium Bedtime Bear, Medium Bedtime Accessories, Small Bitty Pajamas & Bear **Paper** Little Sizzles™ Paper Pad "Pastels", "Earth Tones" and "Rainbow" by Sizzix™; Bitty Gone Big™ "Dad's Plaid" by Provo Craft®; Flesh Cardstock **Miscellaneous** Chalk by Craf-T Products, Scissors, Black Micron Pen .02 by Sakura, Glue Pen by Zig

Tip: This might be a fun card to use as a sleepover party invitation! Just include the who, what, where and when and you're set to go!

Alternative Sayings:
"Hope You're Feeling Better Soon",
"You're Invited to a Sleepover!"

Actual Size: 2-7/8" wide x 3-3/4" high
(measurement includes accessories)

PEPPERMINT CANDY GIRL
DECEMBER

SUPPLY LIST: Sizzix® Dies Large Doll Body, Large Doll Boy Hair #1, Medium Doll Bedtime Bear, Small Candy **Paper** Little Sizzles™ Paper Pad "Pastels", "Watercolors", "Rainbow" and "Earth Tones" by Sizzix™, Bitty Gone Big™ "Cross Your Heart" by Provo Craft® **Miscellaneous** Chalk by Craf-T Products, Clear Wrapping Tissue by Cindus Corporation, Tiny Silver Brad by Deco Fastener, Thin Silver Ribbon by Offray, Scissors, Black Micron Pen .02 by Sakura, Glue Dots, Glue Pen by Zig, Pop Dots by All Night Media

Tip: Trim off the wrapping paper "sides" of the Candy before wrapping in the clear tissue paper. Secure the tissue with Glue Dots. **Tip:** Pierce the tiny brad into the Pajamas only. This way you won't be able to see the brad from the inside of the card. **Tip:** Cut three pieces of the curly Boy Hair. Trim down two of them to make curly ponytails or piggy tails. Place a Pop Dot under the ponytails to add dimension. Secure the ribbon bows under the tops of the ponytails. **Tip:** To make the girl look like she's holding the candy, just trim off her hands and place on top of the candy. The bottom of her pajama sleeves will look like they're her elbows.

Alternative Sayings:
"You're the Sweetest Thing!"
"Sweets for the Sweet this Christmas"

Actual Size: 2-7/8" wide x 3-3/4" high
(measurement includes accessories)

CANDY CANE BOY
DECEMBER

SUPPLY LIST: Sizzix® Dies Large Doll Body, Large Doll Boy Hair #1, Medium Doll Bedtime Bear, Medium Candy Cane **Paper** Little Sizzles™ Paper Pad "Pastels", "Earth Tones" and "Watercolors" by Sizzix™, Bitty Gone Big™ "Cross Your Heart" and "Lost in the Woods" by Provo Craft® **Miscellaneous** Chalk by Craf-T Products, Tiny Silver Brads by Deco Fastener, Thin Silver Ribbon by Offray, Scissors, Black Micron Pen .02 by Sakura, Glue Pen by Zig, Glue Dots

Tip: Pierce your brads through just the pajamas so that they can't be seen from the inside of the card. **Tip:** Trim the crotch of the pajamas up a little (after you place them onto the body so that you can use the legs as a guide), for a different look.

Alternative Sayings:
"Merry Christmas"
"Sorry I bit off more than I could chew"

Actual Size: 2-7/8" wide x 3-3/4" high
(measurement includes accessories)

Chapter
Twelve

PLACE CARDS

PLACE CARDS

The dishes are laid, the glasses are gleaming, the napkins are folded with care. So much of your time has gone into the details of making this a warm and inviting occasion for those that you love. The finishing touch is a handmade place card, letting each guest know that they not only have a place at your table, but also in your heart.

DOUBLE HEART
CARD

SUPPLY LIST: Sizzix® Die Small Heart Double **Paper** Little Sizzles™ Paper Pad "Pastels" and "Rainbow" by Sizzix™ **Miscellaneous** Black Micron Pen .03 by Sakura, Xyron Adhesive

Tip: Cut double hearts on the fold and adhere them together. Then place name on top.

Actual Size: 3" wide x 3" high

EASTER BRUNCH
CARD

SUPPLY LIST: Sizzix® Dies Large Egg Cracked, Small Eggs **Paper** Color Wheel™ "Tropical" by Provo Craft® **Miscellaneous** Alphabitties "Scrapbook White" by Provo Craft®, Eyelets by Doodlebug, Eyelet Setting Tool, Hammer by Bright Ideas, Ribbon by Offray, Easter Grass

Tip: Bend the bottom fourth of the card back to make it stand up on the table.

Actual Size: 2" wide x 3-1/4" high (each)

FOIL FLOWERS
CARD

SUPPLY LIST: Sizzix® Dies Large Squares, Small Flower #1 **Paper** Little Sizzles™ Paper Pad "Pastels" by Sizzix™ **Miscellaneous** Ultra Foil by Reynolds, Bitty Alphabet Template by Provo Craft®, Eyelets by Doodlebug, Eyelet Setting Tool, Hammer by Bright Ideas, Green Metallic Wire by Artistic Wire, Wire Cutter, Wire Pliers, Embossing Stylus, Zig Glue Pen, Glue Dots

Tip: Cut four white cardstock place cards on the fold. Cut four squares of foil to go inside each place card. **Tip:** To emboss your guest's name inside their place card, just hold up the template to the card where you'd like the letters to be placed, then slip it behind the foil in the same position and emboss. (It'll be backwards when you emboss, but on the front it will be facing the right way) **Tip:** To put texture into the centers, just emboss little freehand circles with your stylus.

Alternative Saying:
"Welcome!"

Actual Size: 2" x 2" (each)

STICKER FLOWER
CARD

SUPPLY LIST: Sizzix® Die Large Squares **Paper** Little Sizzles™ Paper Pad "Pastels" by Sizzix™ **Miscellaneous** Vellum Stickers "Friends & Flowers" by Provo Craft®, Yellow Fabric Covered Wire, Wire Cutting Tool, Wire Pliers, Scissors, Black Micron Pen .03 by Sakura, Zig Glue Pen

Tip: Place the stickers on white cardstock and trim around to give them stability. Adhere back of sticker (on cardstock) to smallest Square on the Squares die. Tie cotton covered wire with a little name tag on it around pot, securing with glue between the sticker and the Square. **Tip:** Try this idea with almost any sticker for any occasion! Delight your family by letting your kids help you pick the stickers that apply to each family member to make an ordinary dinner extraordinary!

Actual Size: 1-3/8" wide x 3-1/8" high

Actual Size: 3-1/4" wide x 1" high

CRAYON
CARD

SUPPLY LIST: Sizzix® Die Medium Pencil **Paper** Bitty Scrap Pad "Just Ducky Baby", "Happy Halloween" and "Dots, Squiggles & Speckles" by Provo Craft®; Scrap Pad "Awesome Athletes" by Provo Craft® **Miscellaneous** Clear Alphabitties™ "Wedge Black" by Provo Craft®, Scissors, Black Micron Pen .05 by Sakura, Xyron Adhesive

Tip: What a fun way to welcome your students into the classroom on their first day of school! Or, how about sending this off with your child, tucked away in their lunch box with a special message inside for a noon time surprise! Or for all of those times you thought, "I'd love to let that teacher know how much I appreciate all of her love and hard work", but didn't have quite the right card for the occasion? This card does all of those and more!

WEDDING COUPLE
CARD

SUPPLY LIST: Sizzix® Dies Large Doll Body, Large Doll Girl Hair #1, Large Doll Boy Hair #1, Large Doll Dresses, Large Doll Winter Clothes, Large Doll Overalls **Paper** Little Sizzles™ Paper Pad "Pastels", "Earth Tones" and "Watercolors" by Sizzix™; Color Wheel™ Bitty Scrap Pad "Tropical Palette" and "Sherbet Palette" by Provo Craft®p; Bitty Scrap Pad "Birthday Bash" and "And Summer Too" by Provo Craft®; Scrap Pad "Fish All Day" and "Americana Patchwork" by Provo Craft® **Miscellaneous** Clear Alphabitties™ "Wedge" by Provo Craft®, Chalk by Craf-T Products, Tiny Hole Punch by McGill, Sticker Tweezers by Provo Craft®, Scissors, Black Micron Pen .03 by Sakura, Xyron Adhesive, Zig Glue Pen

Tip: To make the tuxedo, just cut down the top of the snowsuit to make the black tuxedo jacket. Trim down the Overalls to make the pants and use the T-Shirt for his white shirt. Place little details like buttons on the shirt front with your black pen. **Tip:** The necklace and earrings are made from the tiny circle hole punch.

Actual Size: 2-1/2" wide x 3-1/2" high (each)

Mom & Dad
CARD

SUPPLY LIST: Sizzix® Dies Large Doll Body, Large Doll Girl Hair #1, Large Doll Boy Hair #1, Large Doll Dresses, Large Doll Summer Clothes, Small Doll Shoes #1 **Paper** Bitty Scrap Pad "Dots, Squiggles and Speckles", "Calypso Green", "Flamingo Pink" and "Blueberry" by Provo Craft®; Little Sizzles™ Paper Pad by Sizzix™, Flesh Cardstock, **Miscellaneous** Pathways™ "Traditional Black" and "Americana Alphabet Overlays" by Provo Craft®, Scissors, Black Micron Pen .02 by Sakura, Xyron Adhesive

Tip: Be sure and cut the Doll on the fold at the top of the head so that these little place settings can stand on their own. **Tip:** Place the Alphabet Overlays onto white cardstock, then trim around the letters. Trim off the Doll's arms at the shoulders and fold around "Mom" and "Dad". (The clothes will cover the missing arms.) This place setting concept also works well for the names of every guest or member of your family!

Actual Size: 2-3/4" wide x 3-3/4" high

MOM
CARD

SUPPLY LIST: Sizzix® Dies ShadowBox™ Alphabet, Medium Grass **Paper** Bitty Gone Big™ "Cherry Posies" by Provo Craft®, Color Wheel™ Paper "Calypso Green" by Provo Craft® **Miscellaneous** Xyron Adhesive

Tip: Cut out posies from the "Cherry Posies" paper to make the flowers. Cut stems from "Calypso Green" paper. To make a stand for the letters cut a strip of paper 4-1/2" x 2" and fold it in half. Place Grass in front of letters.

Actual Size: 4-3/4" wide x 3-1/4" high

DAD
CARD

SUPPLY LIST: Sizzix® Dies ShadowBox™ Alphabet, Medium Wave, Medium Fishing Pole **Paper** Bitty Gone Big™ "Forever Green", "Pail of Water" and Light and Dark Brown Cardstock by Provo Craft® **Miscellaneous** Twine, Ceramic Fish Embellishment

Tip: Cut the letters using the outside 'shadow' on the fold. The letters are what makes the card stand up. Cut out the Wave and glue it to the inside of the letters.

Actual Size: 3-7/8" wide x 1-1/2" high (not including fishing pole)

PARTY HAT
CARD

SUPPLY LIST: Sizzix® Die Medium Party Hat **Paper** Bitty Scrap Pad "Dots, Squiggles & Speckles" by Provo Craft® **Miscellaneous** Scissors, Black Micron Pen .03 by Sakura, Xyron Adhesive

Tip: This place card can double as a birthday invitation and versatile party thank you note. You could also tie it to a gift bag as a "To/From" tag.

Actual Size: 1-3/4" wide x 2-1/2" high

KITE
CARD

SUPPLY LIST: Sizzix® Die Large Diamond #1 **Paper** Little Sizzles™ Paper Pad "Country" by Sizzix™ **Miscellaneous** Clear Letters "Parlor White" by Provo Craft®, Twine, Green Raffia, Scissors, Black Micron Pen .03 by Sakura, Xyron Adhesive

Tip: Secure the twine between the two layers of paper (inside and outside of card). To finish it off, tie raffia bits around the twine and trim ends. **Tip:** This could double as a super spring party invitation.

Alternative Sayings:
"You Make My Heart Soar"
"You've exceeded my HIGH expectations!"
Tie a little key charm to the twine and say, "Of all the great discoveries, I'm glad I discovered YOU!"

Actual Size: 3-1/2" wide x 4-3/4" high (not including string)

WATERMELON
CARD

SUPPLY LIST: Sizzix® Dies Large Doll Body, Small Watermelon, Small Bitty Dresses, Small Doll Shoes #1 **Paper** Little Sizzles™ "Earth Tones" by Sizzix™, Bitty Gone Big™ "Cross Your Heart" and "Little Boy Blueberry" by Provo Craft®, Fleshtone and White Cardstock, Color Wheel™ Paper "Leaf Green" by Provo Craft® **Miscellaneous** Alphabitties™ "Pixie Serif" Black by Provo Craft®

Tip: Die-cut both the Doll and the Watermelon on the fold. Cut out bite marks from the Watermelon.

Actual Size: 2-1/4" wide 3-3/4" high

102

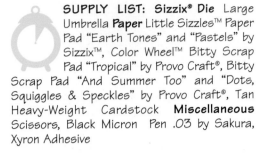

UMBRELLA
CARD

SUPPLY LIST: Sizzix® Die Large Umbrella **Paper** Little Sizzles™ Paper Pad "Earth Tones" and "Pastels" by Sizzix™, Color Wheel™ Bitty Scrap Pad "Tropical" by Provo Craft®, Bitty Scrap Pad "And Summer Too" and "Dots, Squiggles & Speckles" by Provo Craft®, Tan Heavy-Weight Cardstock **Miscellaneous** Scissors, Black Micron Pen .03 by Sakura, Xyron Adhesive

Tip: Use a super heavy-weight cardstock (for strength) to die-cut the Umbrella on the fold. Use the pretty patterned papers to layer on top of the base to make it decoratively "beachy". Tip: Cut a tiny name tag and hang it a little off center so that when the Umbrella tilts as it sits at the place setting, the name is still straight. Mat the name tag with a coordinating paper.

Alternative Sayings:
"Bon Voyage"
"Come to our Beach Party!"
"Thanks for the relaxing time"

Actual Size: 3-5/8" wide x 3-1/2" high

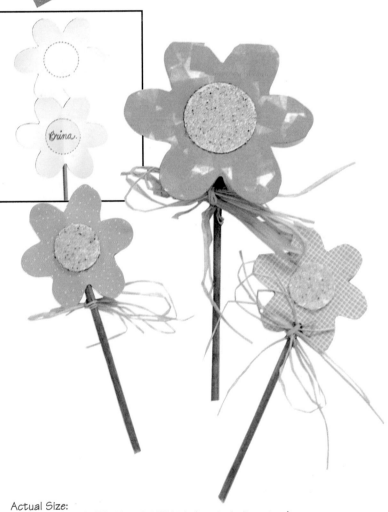

PLANTED DAISIES
CARD

SUPPLY LIST: Sizzix® Die Large Daisy #2 **Paper** Color Wheel™ Bitty Scrap Pad "Lime Sherbet", "Azure Blue", "Lilac Petals" and "Custard" by Provo Craft® **Miscellaneous** Art Accentz™ "Clear Beedz™" by Provo Craft®, Green Ink Pad or Green Paint, Small Dowel, Raffia, Black Micron Pen .03 by Sakura, Art Accentz™ "Terrifically Tacky Tape™ Sheets" by Provo Craft®, Liquid Adhesive by Tombow

Tip: To save your Tacky Tape Sheets, just cut a small portion a little larger than the centers of your Daisies. Place under center of Daisy die and die-cut only the center of the Daisy. Remove one side of the backing and dip into your clear Beedz™. Remove the other side of the backing and attach to the center of Daisies. Tip: Fill the pots with beans, rice or styrofoam with moss to hold the dowels in place.

Alternative Sayings:
"Everything Grows with Love"
"In the Garden of Life, You are the Flowers"

Actual Size:
LARGE FLOWER 3" wide x 2-1/2" high (not including stem)
SMALL FLOWER 2" wide x 2" high

BABY BUGGY
CARD

SUPPLY LIST: Sizzix® Die Baby Carriage **Paper** Bitty Scrap Pad "Ducky Baby Girl" by Provo Craft®, White Cardstock **Miscellaneous** Alphabitties™ "Pixie Serif Sherbet" by Provo Craft®, Flower and Circle Bradletz™ by Provo Craft®, Lace, Scallop Scissors, Black Micron Pen by Sakura

Tip: If the Bradletz™ you want to use aren't quite the right color, paint them to match. Add a small dot to the center of the flower to accent.

Alternative Saying:
"A New Arrival"

Actual Size: 4" wide x 4" high

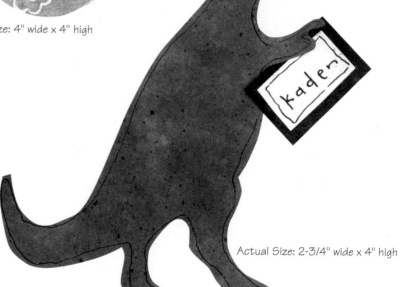

Actual Size: 2-3/4" wide x 4" high

DINOSAUR
CARD

SUPPLY LIST: Sizzix® Die Large Tyrannosaurus Rex **Paper** Little Sizzles™ Paper Pad "Pastels" and "Watercolors" by Sizzix™, Bitty Scrap Pad "Dots, Squiggles and Speckles" by Provo Craft® **Miscellaneous** Chalk by Stampin' Up, Scissors, Black Micron Pen .03 by Sakura, Xyron Adhesive

Tip: Place the black cardstock underneath the dinosaur's eye on the inside of this place card. Chalk his cheeks and make him "hold" the child's name. **Tip:** This is also an easy and age appropriate idea for a child's birthday party invitation or thank you note.

FENCE
CARD

SUPPLY LIST: Sizzix® Die Medium Fence, Picket **Paper** Little Sizzles™ Paper Pad "Pastels" by Sizzix™, Bitty Scrap Pad "French Country" and "Primary Colors" by Provo Craft®, Scrap Pad "Let's Hit the Road" by Provo Craft® **Miscellaneous** Scissors, Black Micron Pen .03 by Sakura, Xyron Adhesive

Tip: Hand cut or punch out the blue flower accent. **Tip:** Remember to cut all place cards on the fold at the top.

Alternative Saying:
"Welcome!"

Actual Size: 3-1/4" wide x 1-3/4" high

FALL WAGON
CARD

Actual Size: 3-1/2" wide x 3-1/2" high

SUPPLY LIST: Sizzix® Dies Medium Wagon, Medium Stars Primitive, Small Pumpkin, Small Cat **Paper** Little Sizzles™ Paper Pad "Rainbow", "Watercolors", "Country" and "Pastels" by Sizzix™ **Miscellaneous** Clear Alphabitties™ "Wedge Black" by Provo Craft®, Ultra Foil "Silver" by Reynolds, Eyelets by Doodlebug, Eyelet Setting Tool, Hammer by Bright Ideas, Green Fabric Covered Wire, Yellow Fabric Covered Wire, Wire Cutting Tool, Wire Pliers, Scissors, Black Micron Pen .03 by Sakura, Xyron Adhesisve

Tip: Die-cut and decorate the front of this place card, then adhere it to a Wagon that has been cut on the fold at the top, out of white cardstock. **Tip:** Place the eyelets in the center of both wheels **Tip:** Thread the yellow fabric covered wire through the tiny Primitive Star for the cat's collar. Wrap the green fabric covered wire around the Pumpkins and twirl with wire pliers or a thin pencil.

Alternative Sayings:
"Join us on a Hay Ride!"
"Happy Halloween"

Actual Size: 4" wide x 1-3/8" high

BAT & STARS
CARD

SUPPLY LIST: Sizzix® Dies Medium Bat, Medium Stars Primitive **Paper** Little Sizzles™ Paper Pad "Watercolors" and "Rainbow" by Sizzix™, Color Wheel™ Bitty Scrap Pad "Crayon Box" by Provo Craft® **Miscellaneous** Tiny Circle Hole Punch by McGill, Black Wire by Artistic Wire, Wire Cutting Tool, Wire Pliers, White Gel Roller Pen by Marvy, Black Micron Pen by Sakura, Xyron Adhesive

Tip: Cut an extra Bat aside from your Bat on the fold to place on top of the front of the folded place card. This allows you to cover up the flat part at the tops of the wings that the fold causes. Secure the wires in between those two layers. You'll have a super strong place card and keepsake that your guests can take home after the party! **Tip:** Outline the Bat shape with the white gel roller pen. Write the name of each guest on the little Star.

Alternative Sayings:
"Happy Halloween" – on the inside of the bat
"I'm going Batty without you!"

GHOST OF HONOR
CARD

Actual Size: 3-1/2" wide x 3-3/4" high

SUPPLY LIST: Sizzix® Dies Large Haunted House, Medium Ghosts **Paper** Little Sizzles™ Paper Pad "Pastels" and "Watercolors" by Sizzix™ **Miscellaneous** Alphabitties™ Clear "Wedge White" by Provo Craft®, Glue Pen by Zig

TURKEY
CARD

SUPPLY LIST: Sizzix® Die Large Turkey **Paper** Little Sizzles™ Paper Pad "Classics" and "Earth Tones" by Sizzix™, Bitty Scrap Pad "Birthday Bash" and "Primary Colors" by Provo Craft® **Miscellaneous** Alphabitties™ "Black Fat Dot" by Provo Craft®, Googly Eyes by Westrim Craft, Scissors, Black Micron Pen .03 by Sakura, Xyron Adhesive

Tip: Place cards add the "extra touch" to your holiday decor. This friendly Turkey will bring color and whimsy to the Thanksgiving table while directing your guests where to park their feathers! **Tip:** Start by cutting the Turkeys with the top center feather on the fold. Overlay and adhere orange Turkey to folded brown Turkey. Trim as shown and overlay the following colored Turkeys: gold onto red, green onto gold and blue onto green. Make folds down the center of the feathers. Trim the legs off the colored feathers and adhere onto the folded Turkey over the orange paper. Cut out the Turkey body from the brown (unfolded) Turkey. Adhere over the feathers and legs. Assemble as shown.

Actual Size: 4" wide x 4-1/2" high

Actual Size LEAVES:
1-1/4" wide x 1-3/4" high

FALL GOURD
CARD

SUPPLY LIST: Sizzix® Die Small Leaf #1 **Paper** Cardstock in various fall colors **Miscellaneous** Pathways™ Alphabitties™ "Green" by Provo Craft®, Mini Pumpkin or Gourd, Wire

Tip: You could use any Sizzix® Leaf on this place card. These are so quick and easy to make yet will receive many compliments.

SNOWMAN
CARD

SUPPLY LIST: Sizzix® Die Large Snowman **Paper** Little Sizzles™ Paper Pad "Pastels", "Watercolors" and "Rainbow" by Sizzix™; Bitty Scrap Pad "Primary Colors" and "French Country Colors" by Provo Craft®; White Cardstock **Miscellaneous** Tiny Circle Hole Punch by McGill, Scissors, Black Micron Pen .03 by Sakura, Xyron Adhesive

Tip: Hand cut a little orange carrot nose for your Snowman. **Tip:** Cut out a little white daisy from one of the decorative papers in the French Country Bitty Scrap Pad and adhere it to the Snowman's hat band. **Tip:** If you have a little more time, try gluing embroidery floss under the edge of the scarf to make "fringe".

Alternative Sayings:
"Let it Snow"
"Happy Holidays"
"You Warm my Heart"
"Sorry I was a little 'Frosty' the other day"

Actual Size:
2-3/4" wide x
3-1/2" high

Actual Size:
3-7/8" wide x
3" high

POINSETTIA
CARD

SUPPLY LIST: Sizzix® Dies Large Squares, Large Daisy #2, Small Leaf #2 **Paper** Little Sizzles™ Paper Pad "Pastels" by Sizzix™, "Red Bananenkordel" and "Green Bananenkordel" by Pulsar **Miscellaneous** Clear Alphabitties™ "Wedge Black" by Provo Craft®, Raffia, Art Accentz™ "Beedz™" by Provo Craft®, Teflon Scissors, Art Accentz™ "Terrifically Tacky Tape™ Sheets" by Provo Craft®, Xyron Adhesive

Tip: Unwrap the Bananenkordel and place through a Xyron machine or glue onto white cardstock. (You'll need to spread out the Bananenkordel as far as it stretches side to side.) Die-cut this sheet of "Bananenkordel paper" using the largest Daisy. Trim the edges of the petals all the way down into the center and back out to the edges of the petals to look like a Poinsettia leaf. Do this to two different Daisies. Use the same technique to adhere the green Bananenkordel to white cardstock and die-cut using the Leaf #2 die. Place the two Poinsettias on top of each other and rotate the top layer. Place the leaves between the two layers and adhere them all together. Bend the top Leaves toward you to create a realistic Poinsettia. **Tip:** Now cut the largest Square on the fold at the top and adhere the Poinsettia to the front of the Square. Cut the largest Square out of a Terrifically Tacky Tape™ Sheet. Remove one layer and place inside of the folded Square. Now remove the other layer and dip into Beedz™. Apply the names of your guests with Alphabitties™ in the inside of the Square over the Beedz.

Alternative Use:
These Poinsettias could also be used to make a beautiful Christmas or Holiday card cover.

FERN
CARD

SUPPLY LIST: Sizzix® Die Medium Fern **Paper** Bitty Scrap Pad "French Country", "Tropical" and "Primary Colors" by Provo Craft® **Miscellaneous** Scissors, Black Micron Pen .03 by Sakura, Xyron Adhesive

Tip: This is a quick and super easy place card that will work for almost any occasion. Imagine it for Spring, Summer, Mother's Day or Father's Day! Just place the names of your guests on the front or inside of the Fern shape. **Tip:** This concept also works as a versatile thank you note. **Tip:** If the fold at the top of the Fern bothers you, simply cut an extra Fern and place it on top of the Fern cut on the fold. Adhere with adhesive.

Actual Size:
1-7/8" wide x
3-3/4" high

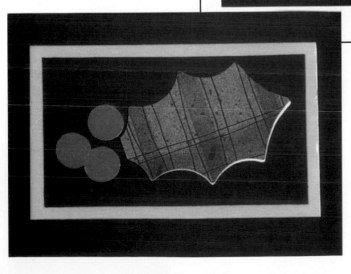

Actual Size:
3" wide x
2-1/4" high

HOLLY
CARD

SUPPLY LIST: Sizzix® Dies Large Rectangle # 1, Large Rectangle #2, Large Holly & Berries **Paper** Little Sizzles™ Paper Pad "Watercolors" and "Classics" by Sizzix™, Color Wheel™ Scrap Pad "Apple Red" by Provo Craft®, Scrap Pad "Winter Holidays" by Provo Craft® **Miscellaneous** Alphabitties™ "Wedge Clear" by Provo Craft®, Scissors, Black Micron Pen .03 by Sakura, Xyron Adhesive

Tip: I love when hostesses have these special kinds of things ready for their guests. Those special little 'extras' that make you feel like the guest of honor. Attention to even tiny detail makes for memories that last forever! **Tip:** To make a smaller place card, just use the Rectangle #2 without matting it onto the Rectangle #1. **Tip:** Crumple red cardstock before die-cutting the berries.

Alternative Saying:
"Merry Christmas!"

Chapter Thirteen

I LOVE YOU CARDS

I LOVE YOU CARDS

Every September 21st, my best friend would, without provocation, send out "St. Vivid's Day" cards to those she loved. When asked, "What in the world is St. Vivid's Day?", she responded sweetly, "St. Vivid was the patron saint of spontaneous acts of love and friendship." She also added that it was the perfect time to send a card because September was particularly lacking in interesting holidays and she needed an excuse to tell people that she thought they were fabulous. Gratefully, we don't need an excuse anymore. It doesn't have to be a holiday, or birthday, or even the typical celebratory event that we often think of as a card giving opportunity. There are just times when a card exchanged between two friends or loved ones will inspire laughter and appreciation. You can almost hear the giggles when they open your gift, and there's just not enough of that in our world.

Actual Size: 2-1/8" wide x 3-1/2" high

I LOVE CHOO
CARD

SUPPLY LIST: Sizzix® Dies Large Train, Medium Hearts **Primitive Paper** Little Sizzles™ Paper Pad "Pastels", "Watercolors" and "Classics" by Sizzix™ **Miscellaneous** Bradletz™ "Primitive Hearts" by Provo Craft®, Black Raffia, Scissors, Black Micron Pen .03 by Sakura, Xyron Adhesive, Glue Pen by Zig

Tip: You can attach the raffia to the Train with eyelets as well as Bradletz™. **Tip:** If you have a hard time finding black raffia, just take a large black marker and color any shade of raffia black!

Alternative Sayings:
"How have choo been lately?"
"My heart skips rails for you"
"You have me trained right!"
"Choo are so sweet!"

I'M ALL YOURS
CARD

SUPPLY LIST: Sizzix® Dies Large Hearts, Large Doll Body, Large Doll Girl Hair #1 **Paper** Little Sizzles™ Paper Pad "Earth Tones" and "Rainbow" by Sizzix™, Flesh Cardstock **Miscellaneous** Clear Alphabitties™ "Wedge White" by Provo Craft®, Art Accentz™ "Purple and Orange Micro Beedz™" by Provo Craft®, Art Accentz™ "Terrifically Tacky Tape™ Sheets" by Provo Craft®, Teflon Scissors, Black Micron Pen .02 by Sakura, Xyron Adhesive

Tip: Cut 3 shapes of the second to largest Heart out of purple cardstock. Cut one shape of the 2nd to largest Heart out of your Terrifically Tacky Tape™ Sheet. After peeling off one layer, dip the sheet into your Beedz™, pressing firmly without touching the sticky side of the sheet with your fingers. Peel off the back layer and attach to the back of the dark purple cardstock. **Tip:** Round the hands off at the wrist with your scissors and place over the beaded heart on the front and purple heart on the inside. The barrette is just a little scrap of Tacky Tape Sheet. With a snip of the scissors here and there, you can trim the Hair to look like the person who is giving or receiving the card!

Alternative Sayings:
"You Have my Heart"
"Happy Valentine's Day"

Have I told 'CHOO' lately how much I LOVE YOU?!

Actual Size: 4-1/4" wide 3-1/4" high

LIFE'S A PICNIC WHEN I'M WITH YOU
CARD

SUPPLY LIST: Sizzix® Die Large Basket, Picnic **Paper** Little Sizzles™ Paper Pad "Earth Tones" by Sizzix™, Bitty Scrap Pad "All Through the Year" by Provo Craft®, Gold Cardstock **Miscellaneous** Red Ribbon by Offray, Red Check Fabric, Fabric Scissors, Black Micron Pen .05 by Sakura, Xyron Adhesive, Glue Pen by Zig, Photo Tape by 3L

Tip: Use photo tape to "hem" the fabric around the edges.

Alternative Saying:
"You're invited to a Picnic Party!"

Actual Size:
5" wide x
3-1/4" high

THANKS
CARD

SUPPLY LIST: Sizzix® Die Large Hearts **Paper** Little Sizzles™ Paper Pad "Pastels" by Sizzix™, Bitty Gone Big™ "Cross Your Heart" by Provo Craft® **Miscellaneous** Clear Alphabitties™ "Pixie Serif Gold" by Provo Craft®, Thin Gold Ribbon by Offray, Gold Eyelets by Doodlebug, Eyelet Setting Tool, Hammer by Bright Ideas, Scissors, Xyron Adhesive

Tip: This quick card can be laced from the top down or from the bottom up, depending on your preference. It's a fun card because it gives the feeling of opening up or unwrapping a present! **Tip:** Use 6 eyelets – 3 on the front and 3 on the inside of the card.

Alternative Saying:
"I Love You With All My Heart"

Actual Size: 2-1/4" wide x 2" high

RIBBON LACED HEART
CARD

SUPPLY LIST: Sizzix® Dies Large Heart #1, Large Heart #2 **Paper** Little Sizzles™ Paper Pad "Pastels" by Sizzix™, Bitty Gone Big™ "Pink Lady" and "Baby Love" by Provo Craft® **Miscellaneous** Clear Alphabitties™ "Wrought Iron Black" by Provo Craft®, Thin White Ribbon by Offray, Small Hole Punch by Provo Craft®, Paper Shaper Scissors "Mini Scallop" by Provo Craft®, Scissors, Black Micron Pen .03 by Sakura, Xyron Adhesive

Tip: To get the hole punches even, mark them with a pencil on the back of your paper, about every 1/8". Lace your ribbon through and tie at the bottom in a bow. Mat on top of the larger Heart and you're done! **Tip:** Try using more traditional male colors and wrapping the smaller Heart with twine or raffia for a more masculine look.

Alternative Saying:
"Happy Anniversary"

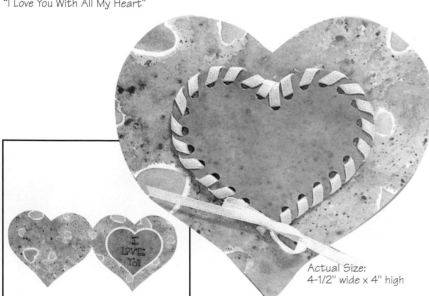

Actual Size:
4-1/2" wide x 4" high

110

Actual Size: 7-1/2" wide x 4-3/8" high

YOU MAKE MY HEART RACE
CARD

SUPPLY LIST: Sizzix® Dies Medium Border Road & Wavy , Small Bunny, Small Turtle **Paper** Little Sizzles™ Paper Pad "Earth Tones" and "Pastel" by Sizzix™ **Miscellaneous** Tiny Googly Eyes, Black Micron Pen .03 by Sakura, Zig Glue Pen

Tip: It's fun to play around with the dies to make them look like they're in motion. Cut green cardstock on the fold at the top of the Turtle's shell. (Place green cardstock back to back if you'd like the center of the card to be green.) Now cut another green cardstock AND green patterned paper for the top of the Turtle. Use these last two to "dress the die" by cutting just the shell off of the plaid turtle and placing in on the plain green Turtle. Now place the "dressed" Turtle on top of the folded Turtle, skewing it slightly to the right so that the turtle has four legs and looks like he's walking. Trim the excess off of the back folded Turtle and you have a Turtle in motion! **Tip:** Try outlining portions or the complete die to define its shape. **Tip:** To make a "track" for the rabbit and tortoise to move across, just cut two slits along the perforation of the Road & Wavy Border Die. Don't cut all the way to the end. This will be the "track" for the dies to move on. Next, make two flat "rings" that fit around the track. They need to overlap on one side so that you can stick them together. Use a heavy duty cardstock so they are durable and will withstand lots of traveling. Next, glue your Turtle and Bunny to their rings. Now they can pass each other depending on your message inside the card!

Alternative Sayings:
"Hope You Have a Speedy Recovery!"
"Way to Hang in There!"
"Thanks for Taking the Time to Stop and Listen"

YOU HOLD THE KEY TO MY HEART
CARD

SUPPLY LIST: Sizzix® Dies Large Hearts, Large Tags, Small Handprint **Paper** Little Sizzles™ Paper Pad "Classics" by Sizzix™, Flesh Cardstock **Miscellaneous** Pathways™ Alphabitties "Traditional Black" by Provo Craft®, White Wired Ribbon by Offray, Silver "Key" Charm, Small Hole Punch, Scissors, Xyron Adhesive, Pop Dots by All Night Media, Glue Dots

Tip: Run both the burgundy plaid and burgundy heart paper through the Xyron adhesive. Place the burgundy plaid paper back to the burgundy heart paper back. Fold and die-cut with the Tag making sure that the heart paper is facing the right way when you open the Tag from the top as shown. **Tip:** Adjust the fingers to "hold" the key with Glue Dots. Place a Glue Dot under the key to secure it to the card. **Tip:** Mat the back of the Tag after it is finished with burgundy cardstock.

Alternative Saying:
"The Key to my Heart is in Your Hand"

Actual Size: 4" wide x 1-7/8" high

"I Love You"
CARD

SUPPLY LIST: Sizzix® Dies Large Squares, Medium Hearts Primitive **Paper** Little Sizzles™ Paper Pad "Watercolors" and "Classics" by Sizzix™, Color Wheel™ Scrap Pad "Black Cherry" and "Wild Rose" by Provo Craft®, White Cardstock **Miscellaneous** Coluzzle® Card & Envelope Template, Cutting Mat and Guarded® Swivel Knife by Provo Craft®, Rectangle and Square Punch by Family Treasures; White Wire by Artistic Wire; Eyelets by Doodlebug; Eyelet Setting Tool; Hammer by Bright Ideas;, Black Seed Beads; Cream Thin Twine; Wire Pliers; Wire Cutter; Scissors; Black Micron Pen .05 by Sakura; Xyron Adhesive; Liquid Adhesive by Tombow

Tip: Looking for a contemporary card to express your love? Great for Valentine's Day, Anniversary or "Just Because", this card says it all. It could even be framed and used as wall art! **Tip:** Glue the seed beads, thread the twine and apply the wire in a swirl to your Hearts before putting the Hearts onto the black Squares. This way, you won't see where they're threaded or attached from the back. **Tip:** Use another Square with a Heart on it to seal the back of the envelope!

Alternative Sayings:
"Happy Anniversary"
"I Miss You"
"Happy Valentine's Day"

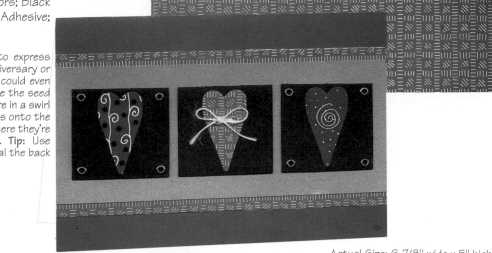

Actual Size: 6-7/8" wide x 5" high

Actual Size:
3" wide x 4-1/4" high

YOU MEAN THE WORLD TO ME
CARD

SUPPLY LIST: Sizzix® Dies Large Squares, Large Circles **Paper** Little Sizzles™ Paper Pad "Watercolors" by Sizzix™, Bitty Gone Big™ "Calm Waters" by Provo Craft® **Miscellaneous** Clear Alphabitties™ "Wedge Black" by Provo Craft®, Watercolor Pencils by Gallery, Small Waterbrush by Niji, Green Writer by Zig, Xyron Adhesive

Tip: Look at a world map and hand trace the continents in pencil before outlining in green pen. Color the inside edges of each continent with green watercolor pencil, then smooth with a small waterbrush. This will give you a soft, grassy look. **Tip:** To make your Alphabitties™ line up, place them along the top of your Alphabitty package, only securing the bottom fifth of each letter. Feel free to overlap each letter, so that you can pull off the entire phrase in one piece.

Alternative Sayings:
"Happy Anniversary"
"My world revolves around YOU!"
"You are the center of my Universe"

I LOVE YOU WITH ALL MY HEARTS
CARD

SUPPLY LIST: Sizzix® Die Small Heart Double **Paper** Little Sizzles™ Paper Pad "Pastels" by Sizzix™, Color Wheel™ Scrap Pad "Wild Rose" by Provo Craft®, Pathways™ Scrap Pad "Illuminations" by Provo Craft®, White Cardstock **Miscellaneous** Pathways™ Clear Alphabitties™ "Illumination Multi" by Provo Craft®, Scissors, Black Micron Pen .03 by Sakura, Xyron Adhesive, Glue Pen by Zig

Tip: Mat the white background with the Wild Rose paper, then mount it onto the heart patterned paper. **Tip:** To make the accordion folded Hearts in the inside, keeping both sides of the paper inside of the cutting blade. Remember — only fold paper two times. Connect both accordion sections in the middle.

Alternative Saying:
"My Heart is Full of Love"

Actual Size: 4-1/4" wide x 4-3/4" high

I LOVE YOU SEW MUCH
CARD

SUPPLY LIST: Sizzix® Die Large Squares **Paper** Little Sizzles™ Paper Pad "Pastels" and "Watercolors" by Sizzix™ **Miscellaneous** Clear Alphabitties™ "Parlor Black" by Provo Craft®, Paper Shaper Scissors "Mini Scallop" by Provo Craft®, Sheer Ribbon by Offray, Sewing Buttons by Dress It Up, Silver Stretchy Twine, Scissors, Black Micron Pen .03 by Sakura, Xyron Adhesive, Glue Dots

Tip: This card is "sew" easy to make! Just cut five large Squares, adhere them onto black cardstock and trim around each of them with your Mini Scallop Scissors. Make sure you leave plenty of room on the black cardstock — it's a lot easier to use decorative scissors when you have at least 1" of paper for the scissors to "grab". Glue on buttons, stick on Alphabitty words, wrap with a ribbon and you're done!

Alternative Sayings:
"I'm "sew" glad we're friends"
"Thank You SEW much!"

WITH ALL MY HEARTS!

Actual Size:
2-1/4" wide x
2-1/4" high (each)

113

YOU'RE THE GLUE THAT STICKS US TOGETHER
CARD

SUPPLY LIST: Sizzix® Die Medium Baby Bottle **Paper** Little Sizzles Paper Pad "Pastels" and "Rainbow" by Sizzix™, Bitty Gone Big "When the Wind Blows" by Provo Craft®, Bitty Color Wheel™ Cardstock Scrap Pad "Crayon Box" by Provo Craft®, Black Shiny Cardstock **Miscellaneous** Clear Alphabitties™ "Parlor White" by Provo Craft®", White Foam by Polyfoam, "White Pearl Iridescent" Fabric Paint by Polymark, Crimper by Provo Craft®, Scissors, Black Micron Pen .03 by Sakura, Xyron Adhesive

Tip: Trim down the tip and the cap of the Baby Bottle to look like a glue container. Crimp the cap. **Tip:** Just fold the blue patterned Little Sizzle sheet in half to make this card. **Tip:** If you're not confident with free handing the loops with the fabric paint, just draw a light line to follow. The paint "glue" will dry over it. Let the paint "glue" dry completely (overnight) before sending.

Alternative Saying:
"Thanks for helping me out of the Sticky Situation"

Actual Size: 3-1/2" wide x 4-3/4" high

YOU PUT THE BOUNCE IN MY STEP
CARD

SUPPLY LIST: Sizzix® Dies Small Basketball, Small Doll Sports Gear **Paper** Little Sizzles™ Paper Pad "Rainbow" and "Watercolors" by Sizzix™, Color Wheel™ Cardstock Scrap Pad "Crayon Box" by Provo Craft®, White Cardstock **Miscellaneous** Clear Alphabitties™ "Wedge Black" by Provo Craft®; Alphabitties™ "Block Black Uppercase" and "Block Black (lowercase)" by Provo Craft®; Bitty Block Letter Frames "Crayon Box Blocks" by Provo Craft®; Coluzzle® Card & Envelope Template, Cutting Mat and Guarded® Swivel Knife by Provo Craft®; Scissors; Black Micron Pen .05 by Sakura, Xyron Adhesive; Pop Dot by All Night Media

Tip: Use the Coluzzle® Card & Envelope Template to cut the card & envelope. Use the smallest 2" x 2" card to make the window on the front of the card. Place the negative cut out from this window onto a black piece of cardstock and use it to make a frame around your window. Use the Coluzzle® 2" x 2" card to cut out the inside of this frame. Be careful to put a lot of pressure onto the template to keep this little piece from sliding. **Tip:** Place a Pop Dot behind the Basketball in the center of your window. Use the small Doll Sports Gear Basketball to seal the envelope. **Tip:** Overlap and jumble the Bitty Block Letter Frames so that you can fit the word "Bounce" across the page.

Alternative Saying:
"Congratulations on the big Game!"

Actual Size: 4" wide x 6" high

For You
Card

SUPPLY LIST: Sizzix® Dies Large Jar & Label, Small Heart Double **Paper** Little Sizzles™ Paper Pad "Pastels" and "Watercolors" by Sizzix™, Silver Metallic Paper **Miscellaneous** Alphabitties™ "Pink Kids" by Provo Craft®, Fibers by Scrappin' Essentials, Primitive Heart Bradletz™ by Provo Craft®, Pink Embroidery Floss by DMC, Needle

Tip: Trim down the Label for the Jar to make a smaller, more delicate tag. **Tip:** I love this idea because of the wonder it creates when the recipient realizes that there are little notes written on each Heart inside the Jar. Just leave the top of the Jar open so that the lucky recipient can shake the love notes out and feel your love Heart by Heart.

Alternative Sayings:
"Lots of Love"
"I love you with all of my hearts!"

Actual Size:
2-3/4" wide x 4" high

Actual Size: 2-1/4" wide x 2" high

I Love You Heart
Card

SUPPLY LIST: Sizzix® Die Large Hearts **Paper** Little Sizzles™ Paper Pad "Pastels" by Sizzix™, Bitty Gone Big™ "Cross Your Heart" by Provo Craft® **Miscellaneous** Clear Alphabitties™ "Pixie Serif Gold" by Provo Craft®, Thin Gold Ribbon by Offray, Gold Eyelets by Doodlebug, Eyelet Setting Tool, Hammer by Bright Ideas, Scissors, Xyron Adhesive

Alternative Sayings:
"I Love You"
"With All My Heart"

I Love You
Card

SUPPLY LIST: Sizzix® Die Small Heart #2 **Paper** Pathways™ Scrap Pad "Illuminations" by Provo Craft® **Miscellaneous** Pathways™ Alphabitties™ "Illuminations" by Provo Craft®, Fibers by Scrappin' Essentials, Scissors, Glue Pen by Zig

Tip: Line your Heart with glue pen to attach the fibers. Hand cut the arrow.

Alternative Saying:
"You've Stolen My Heart"

Actual Size: 4-1/2" wide x 5-1/2" high

115

Chapter Fourteen

My Heart Goes Out To You

SYMPATHY

Difficult times don't come only when someone passes away. We face many trials throughout our lives and it's wonderful to know that we have people who care and are ready to help us through those times. Often we don't need to say anything, but just be a listening presence. Other times, a card can say what spoken words cannot. A sympathy card can soften someone's burden, just by letting them know that you're there.

Actual Size: 6" wide x 4" high

THINKING OF YOU DURING THIS DIFFICULT TIME
CARD

SUPPLY LIST: Sizzix® Die Small Flower #1 **Paper** Pathways Scrap Pad "Romance" by Provo Craft®, Brown and Pink Cardstock, **Miscellaneous** Font: "PC Kennedy" Fontmania PC HugWare™ CD by Provo Craft®, Chalk by Craf-T Products, Silver Jump Rings by John H Bead Company, Craft Knife by Provo Craft®, Small Hole Punch by Provo Craft®, Scissors, Xyron Adhesive

Tip: Cut a rectangle out of patterned paper large enough to hold three Flowers on the front. Cut out three squares with your craft knife to "frame" the Flowers. After cutting three pink Flowers on the fold, attach them to the top of the patterned paper squares with your jump rings. Mat onto a larger piece of brown cardstock.

Alternative Saying:
"We're here for you"

WITH DEEPEST SYMPATHY
CARD

SUPPLY LIST: Sizzix® Dies Medium Leaf, Stem; Small Flower #1 **Paper** Designer Paper "Wedding Set" by Provo Craft®, Scrap Pad "Fish All Day" by Provo Craft®, Cream and Yellow Textured Cardstock **Miscellaneous** Font: "PC Sketched" (download from internet wwwpccrafter.com); Coluzzle® Card and Envelope Template, Cutting Mat and Guarded® Swivel Knife by Provo Craft®; Chalk by Craf-T Products; Paper Trimmer; Scissors; Adhesive Tabs by Pioneer; Liquid Adhesive by Tombow

Actual Size: 6" wide x 4" high

Alternative Saying:
This card also simply says, "I Love You".

DAISY
CARD

SUPPLY LIST: Sizzix® Dies Large Rectangle Frame, Small Daisy #1 **Paper** Bitty Scrap Pad "Dots, Squiggles & Speckles", "Simply School" and "Crackled Antiques/ Faux Finishes" by Provo Craft®; Vellum **Miscellaneous** Font: "PC Callihan" Fontmania PC HugWare™ CD by Provo Craft®, Scissors, Xyron Adhesive

Tip: Xyron the Daisy directly onto the back of the vellum. **Tip:** Place a patterned green sheet in the center of this card to write your sentiment.

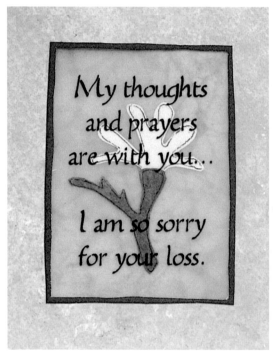

Actual Size: 3-3/4" wide x 4-5/8" high

FOLDED ROSES
CARD

SUPPLY LIST: Sizzix® Dies Large Hearts; Medium Leaf, Stem **Paper** Bitty Color Wheel™ Scrap Pad "Black Cherry", "Ivory Coast" and "Thru the Year" by Provo Craft®; Dark Green Vellum; Vellum **Miscellaneous** Clear Alphabitties™ "Pixie Serif" by Provo Craft®, Ivory Bradletz™ by Provo Craft®, Scissors, Black Micron Pen .02 by Sakura, Xyron Adhesive, Glue Dots

Tip: After Xyroning the black cherry cardstock back to back, die-cut 11 or 12 of the smallest Heart on the Hearts die. Fold 7 of these Hearts as shown, from the top toward the bottom. Adhere these onto the Ivory Coast paper in the shape of a rose. Use Glue Dots to secure the thicker pieces down. Cut 2 Leaf Stems, trimming one down to only one leaf and the stem. Hand cut a stem for the rose bud. Mat with dark green paper. **Tip:** Place a dark green vellum sheet onto the inside of the card. Secure with 4 Ivory Coast Bradletz™ of your choice. Print a sentiment onto a clear sheet of vellum to cut and place in the center or, handwrite your own sentiment onto clear vellum to place in the center.

Alternative Saying:
"Our Thoughts and Prayers are with You"

Actual Size: 4-3/4" wide x 6-7/8" high

BROKEN HEART
CARD

SUPPLY LIST: Sizzix® Dies Large Heart #2 , Large Squares **Paper** Little Sizzles™ Paper Pad "Pastels" and "Country" by Sizzix™, White Cardstock **Miscellaneous** Lavender Embroidery Floss by DMC, Needle, Embossing Stylus, Glue Pen by Zig, Pop Dots by All Night Media

Alternative Saying:
"You've mended my broken heart"

Actual Size: 4-1/2" wide x 4-1/2" high

118

FERN
CARD

SUPPLY LIST: Sizzix® Dies Large Rectangle #1, Medium Fern **Paper** Color Wheel™ Bitty Scrap Pad "Liberty Blue" by Provo Craft®, Bitty Scrap Pad "French Country" by Provo Craft® **Miscellaneous** Font: "PC Becca Brush" (Little Images) PC HugWare™ CD by Provo Craft®, Deco Fasteners by HyGlo, Paper Trimmer, Scissors, Micron Pen .02 by Sakura, Xyron Adhesive

Tip: Print the message on the vellum in dark blue ink and attach it to the base card with tiny gold fasteners. To hide these brads, just place another sheet of coordinating patterned paper back to back with the front of the card. **Tip:** Lightly line the ferns with a black Micron Pen.

Alternative Uses:
This card could be used for many different purposes: Father's Day, Friendship, Thank you, etc.

May peace soon replace the sorrow you feel ... I'm here for you always.

Actual Size:
3-5/8" wide x 5" high

Our Thoughts and prayers are with you......

Actual Size:
3-5/8" wide x 5" high

MY HEART GOES OUT TO YOU
CARD

SUPPLY LIST: Sizzix® Dies Large Jelly Frame, Small Leaf #1 Tiny, Small Leaf #1 **Paper** Little Sizzles™ Paper Pad "Rainbow" by Sizzix™, Vellum **Miscellaneous** Alphabitties™ "Pixie Serif Black" by Provo Craft®, Bradletz™ "Spring Green Primitive Heart" by Provo Craft®, Chalks by Craf-T Products, Fibers by On The Surface

Tip: Jelly Frame is placed on top of a card folded from leaf paper

Alternative Sayings:
"I'm Here For You"
"Let Love Help to Heal your Heart"

My Heart Goes Out To You

Actual Size:
3-1/4" wide x 4" high

ROSE BUDS
CARD

SUPPLY LIST: Sizzix® Dies Large Rectangle #1, Medium Rose **Paper** Little Sizzles™ Paper Pad "Rainbow" and "Watercolors" by Sizzix™, Bitty Gone Big™ "Cross Your Heart Plaid" and "Sweetheart Speckles" by Provo Craft® **Miscellaneous** Scissors, Black Micron Pen .03 by Sakura, Xyron Adhesive, Pop Dots by All Night Media

Tip: Cut an extra Rose out of black cardstock to "shadow" the Roses on the cover of this card. To add dimension, cut an extra 2 rosebuds, and pop just the left side with a Pop Dot. Mat with black cardstock.

Alternative Saying:
This card also simply says, "I Love You".

Chapter Fifteen

Miscellaneous Cards

Miscellaneous Cards

I read an email a few months ago, about a woman who was 83 years old and looking back at her life. She had learned that whenever possible, life should be a pattern of experiences to savor, not to endure. she relayed that she wasn't 'saving' anything; she used the good china for every special event such as losing a pound, getting the sink unstuck or the first Amaryllis blossom. Recognizing these moments and cherishing them is the secret to living wildly in the now and finding sweetness all around you. Lately, I've been taking her advice, using all of the beautiful ribbons that I've collected, never using because they were so collectable. Now they're incorporated in all sorts of cards for every purpose that I can think of: from a pillow shaped card saying, "Thanks for letting us borrow your blow up mattress"; to a seashell with a pearl inside saying, "I treasure our friendship". All of the little things left uncherished or unappreciated and the cards left unsent, those are the things I think I'll regret when I'm 83.

EVERY CLOUD HAS A SILVER LINING
CARD

SUPPLY LIST: Sizzix® Dies Large Cloud#2, Small Cloud #1 **Paper** Bitty™ Scrap Pad "Crackled Antiques/ Faux Finishes" by Provo Craft®, White Cardstock **Miscellaneous** Font: "Rebs Writ" (download from internet www.pccrafter.com) by Provo Craft®, Chalk by Craf-T Products, Xyron Adhesive

Tip: Xyron the silver paper to silver paper, back to back. Fold and die-cut your Large Cloud. Cut a separate blue mottled Cloud and place on top of the front of your large silver cloud. Add smaller Clouds and sayings and you've made someone's day in five minutes.

Actual Size: 5-1/4" wide x 3-1/4" high

HAVE A DAISY OF A DAY
CARD

SUPPLY LIST: Sizzix® Dies Large Squares, Large Daisy #2 **Paper** Little Sizzles™ Paper Pad "Country" and "Pastels" by Sizzix™, Vellum **Miscellaneous** Alphabitties™ "Block Black" Uppercase and Lowercase by Provo Craft®, Craft Knife by Provo Craft®, Hole Punch by Provo Craft®, Yellow Raffia, Scissors, Black Micron Pen .03 by Sakura, Yellow Dotta-Riffic Pen by Zig, Xyron Adhesive

Tip: With a craft knife, cut little slits into the sides of the blue squares. Thread the raffia through these before adhering to your patterned base. This way, you won't be able to see the raffia from the inside. **Tip:** Tie little knots to place at the corners of your vellum sheet inside. Line the vellum sheet with your black pen. Use the Dotta-Riffic pen to make tiny little dots on your yellow Daisy centers.

Alternative Use:
This versatile card could be used for any occasion!

Actual Size: 6-7/8" wide x 5" high

I'VE GOT GREAT NEWS! OR THE CAT'S OUT OF THE BAG!
CARD

SUPPLY LIST: Sizzix® Dies Large Balloons #2, Small Cat **Paper** Little Sizzles™ Paper Pad "Earth Tones" and "Watercolors" by Sizzix™, Bitty™ Gone Big™ "Pink Lady" by Provo Craft® **Miscellaneous** Square Bradletz™ by Provo Craft®, Chalk by Craf-T Products, Craft Knife by Provo Craft®. Thin White Ribbon by Offray, Black Wire by Artistic Wire, Clear Bead and Jewelry Cord by Pepperell Braiding Company, Large Needle, Cosmetic Charms, Wire Cutters, Wire Pliers, Scissors, Black Micron Pen .03 by Sakura, Glue Pen by Zig, Glue Dots

Tip: Use the large round Balloon to make the purse. Cut out the handle portion with a craft knife. It's easier if you draw a fine pencil line to follow. **Tip:** Cut the Cat on the fold from the bottom so that when you pull it out of the bag, you can read the "Call Me! I can't wait to tell you the big news!" **Tip:** Before placing black cardstock in back of the Cat's eyes and nose, wind the black wire through the Cat's nose and secure in back by twisting it and placing a Glue Dot under it. Now line with black cardstock to hold it in place. **Tip:** Attach the charms with clear jewelry cording and a large needle.

Alternative Use:
This might be a fun way to tell relatives the news that you're expecting a long awaited baby! Try modifying the bag with pouches to look more like a baby bag!

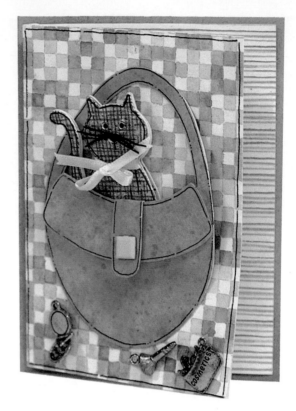

Actual Size: 3-1/2" wide x 4-5/8" high

BON VOYAGE
CARD

SUPPLY LIST: Sizzix® Dies Large Sailboat, Medium Wave, Small Bitty Body, Small Bitty Girl Hair #1, Small Bitty Boy Hair #1, Small Bitty Overalls, Small Bitty Swimsuit, Small Bitty Shorts & Top **Paper** Little Sizzles™ Paper Pad "Classics", "Watercolors" and "Earth Tones" by Sizzix™; Color Wheel™ Scrap Pad "Calypso Green" and " Bahama Blue" by Provo Craft®; Color Wheel™ Cardstock Scrap Pad "Crayon Box" by Provo Craft®; 8-1/2 x 11 White and Flesh Cardstock **Miscellaneous** Alphabitties™ "Fat Dot Multicolored" by Provo Craft®, Chalk by Craf-T Products, Scissors, Black Micron Pen .05 by Sakura, Xyron Adhesive, Glue Pen by Zig

Tip: Place a piece of blue patterned paper back to back. Fold the paper. Cut the Waves at the fold on the bottom of the Wave. Now shift the inside layer a little to the right or left so that the white background shows through just a little. Glue both sheets together. This is the base for your card. Now cut your Sailboat on the fold along the bottom. Tuck and glue into the folded Wave. **Tip:** Cut three Sailboats: one each of Apple Red, White and Sunflower Yellow. Trim the yellow for the stripe on the boat and the stripe for the sail. Glue these on and you're ready to set sail! **Tip:** Try lining the sail and inside of the boat with a black pen. It looks "sewn" when you break up the lines with little II's or X's.

Alternative Sayings:
"Bon Voyage"
"Way to Take Off!"
"Happy Anniversary to the Captain of our Ship! Love, Your First Mate!"

Actual Size: 4-1/4" wide x 4" high

Actual Size: 3-1/4" wide x 4-1/2" high

FAIRY
CARD

SUPPLY LIST: Sizzix® Dies Small Bitty Body, Small Bitty Girl Hair #1, Large Doll Dresses, Medium Butterfly #3 **Paper** Little Sizzles™ Paper Pad "Pastels" and "Watercolors" by Sizzix™, Tan and Flesh Cardstock, Vellum **Miscellaneous** Alphabitties "Parlor" and "Sherbet" by Provo Craft®, Chalk by Craf-T Products, Raffia (for wand handle), Metallic Thread, Art Accentz™ "Treasure Beadz™" by Provo Craft®, Art Accentz™ "Teriffically Tacky Tape™" by Provo Craft®, Pop-Dots by All Night Media

Tip: Cut the arms off the Doll Body and attach them with Bradletz™ so the arms move up and down. Tie metallic thread to the arms (behind the doll) so when pulled the arms appear to "fly". Attach the Doll to the card with Pop Dots to make it stand out.

ANYTHING'S POSSIBLE
CARD

SUPPLY LIST: Sizzix® Dies Large Jar & Label, Large Tags **Paper** Little Sizzles™ Paper Pad "Pastels" and "Earth Tones" by Sizzix™ **Miscellaneous** Alphabitties™ "Rope" by Provo Craft®, Chalk by Craf-T Products, Cork by Craf-T Products, Hole Punch by Provo Craft®, Thin Twine, Scissors, Black Micron Pen .03 by Sakura, Brown Writer Pen by Zig, Xyron Adhesive, Glue Pen by Zig

Tip: Use the tag on the Jar & Label Die to make the cork for the bottle. Just trim the sides a little so that the sides graduate out instead of coming straight up. **Tip:** Place the ship sticker onto white cardstock. Trim around sticker, cutting off everything except the main mast. This way it fits perfectly into the bottle!

Alternative Saying:
"Congratulations! Your ship has come in!"

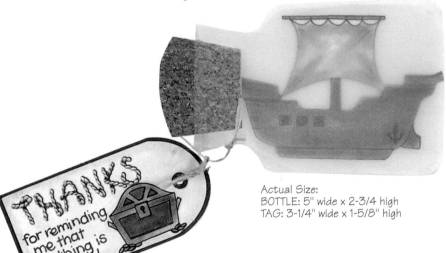

Actual Size:
BOTTLE: 5" wide x 2-3/4 high
TAG: 3-1/4" wide x 1-5/8" high

TULIP GARDEN
CARD

SUPPLY LIST: Sizzix® Die Medium Tulip **Paper** Little Sizzles™ Paper Pad "Watercolors" by Sizzix™ **Miscellaneous** Heart Bradletz™ by Provo Craft®, Magic Mesh by Avant CARD, Small Hole Punch by Provo Craft®, Paper Trimmer, Scissors, Xyron Adhesive

Tip: An easy way to attach a Bradletz™ is to punch a tiny hole in the paper with either a small hole punch or the tip of your scissors. **Tip:** Cut the Tulip stems off at the bottom of the card.

Alternative Use:
This is another versatile card that could be used as gift stationery.

Actual Size:
4-3/4" wide
x 3-1/2" high

CAMERA
CARD

Actual Size: 2-1/2" wide x 2" high (folded)

SUPPLY LIST: Sizzix® Die Medium Camera **Paper** Bitty Scrap Pad "Birthday Bash" by Provo Craft®, Black Cardstock **Miscellaneous** Scissors, Gold Pen, Liquid Adhesive by Tombow

Tip: Fold black cardstock into two sections with folds just on the inside of each side of the Camera die. (These folds will be about 2" apart.) Decide how many folds you would like: one for 1-2 photos, two for 2-3 photos or three for 3-4 photos. Die-cut Cameras. Print or write sayings onto yellow star paper. Saying should only be about 1" length or width. Trace 2 circles of the yellow star paper (using the perforated lines on the outer part of the Camera 'lens', centering the saying. Glue one on front of Camera, and if desired, glue one on the back of front of Camera. (This space could also be used for another photo.) Using liquid adhesive, adhere other pictures on other Cameras. With a gold pen, carefully trace around perforated lines on the Camera. Draw 2 or 3 stars around the circles. **Tip:** Try laminating this entire card to send to the Grandparents for a Grandma & Grandpa's Brag Book!

Alternative Sayings:
"The "PICS" of the Litter!"
"Look What You've Been Missing!"

DREAMS . . .
MAY YOURS COME TRUE
CARD

SUPPLY LIST: Sizzix® Dies Large Tags, Large Squares, Small Dragonfly ,**Paper** Little Sizzles™ Paper Pad "Watercolors" by Sizzix™, 8-1/2" x 11 White Cardstock, Vellum **Miscellaneous** Clear Alphabitties™ "Wrought Iron Black" by Provo Craft®, Clear Letter Stickers "Wrought Iron Black" by Provo Craft®, Chalk by Craf-T Products, Black Wire by Artistic Wire, Black Eyelets by Doodlebug, Wire Cutting Tool, Wire Pliers, Eyelet Setting Tool, Hammer by Bright Ideas, Scissors, Black Micron Pen .03 by Sakura, Xyron Adhesive

Tip: Cut three layers of vellum Dragonflies at one time. Place one under the black body on the first Tag, a few under the body on the second Tag, and many under the body on the third Tag. Bend them upwards to look as if they're in flight **Tip:** Use green and pink chalk to dust the edges of the front and Squares on the inside of this card.

Alternative Sayings:
"HOPE"
"LOVE"

Actual Size: 7-1/2" wide x 5" high

A + Teacher
Card

SUPPLY LIST: Sizzix® Die Medium Pencil **Paper** Little Sizzles™ Paper Pad "Watercolors" and "Earth Tones" by Sizzix™, Color Wheel™ Cardstock Scrap Pad "Crayon Box" and "Tropical" by Provo Craft®, Bitty Gone Big™ "In The Meadow" by Provo Craft® **Miscellaneous** Clear Alphabitties™ "Pixie Serif" by Provo Craft®, Clear Letters "Pixie Serif" by Provo Craft®, Silver Ultra Foil by Reynolds, Square Bradletz™ by Provo Craft®, Yellow Eyelet by Doodlebug, Eyelet Setting Tool, Hammer by Simple Ideas, Scissors, Black Micron Pen .03 by Sakura, Xyron Adhesive

Tip: When making the Pencil portion of this card, remember to place yellow paper on the fold a little to the left of the right side of the die design. It's easy to add all of the layers of the Pencil onto the yellow base. The order should go: 1. eraser, 2. foil, 3. wood, 4. lead tip. **Tip:** Tie the ribbon closure on the Pencil before adhering it onto the front of the card. **Tip:** To get a super crinkly look to your cardstock, get it completely wet, crinkle and let dry overnight.

Alternative Saying:
"You Make the Grade!"

Actual Size: 5-1/2" wide x 3-3/4" high

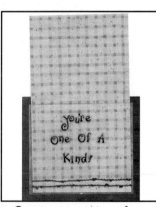

You're One of a Kind!
Card

SUPPLY LIST: Sizzix® Dies Large Rectangle #1, Large Tags, Large Squares **Paper** Bitty Gone Big™ "Stained Grass", "Pink Lady" and "Plum Pie" by Provo Craft® **Miscellaneous** Pathways™ Clear Alphabitties™ "Traditional Black" by Provo Craft®, Heart Bradletz™ by Provo Craft®, Tiny Silver Brad by Deco Fastener, Fibers by On the Surface, Craft Knife by Provo Craft®, Scissors, Black Micron Pen .03 by Sakura, Pink Writer Pen by Zig, Xyron Adhesive, Glue Pen by Zig

Tip: Try using the small Tag and the large Square to make these purses! By trimming the Square diagonally and trimming the Tag from the top, you can make custom purses and bags to make any girlie girl card! **Tip:** Tuck fibers underneath the green patterned paper so that your edges won't fray. Secure with a glue pen.

Alternative Sayings:
Adjust the greetings to make Friendship or Mother's Day cards, or even a "You're my Bag Baby!"

Actual Size: 4-7/8" wide x 4-1/8" high

DON'T FORGET TO WRITE
CARD

SUPPLY LIST: Sizzix® Dies Large Cloud #2, Medium Airplane, Medium Banner, Small Cloud #1, Small Bitty Body, Small Bitty Girl Hair #1, Small Bitty Boy Hair #1, Small Bitty Overalls, Small Bitty Shorts & Top **Paper** Little Sizzles™ Paper Pad "Pastels" by Sizzix™, Color Wheel™ Cardstock Scrap Pad "Crayon Box" by Provo Craft®, Color Wheel™ Scrap Pad "Bahama Blue" by Provo Craft® **Miscellaneous** Clear Alphabitties™ "Pixie Serif Black" by Provo Craft®, Chalk by Craf-T Products, Sticker Tweezers by Provo Craft®, Embossing Gun by Marvy Uchida, White Opaque Embossing Powder by Stamp-n Stuff, Red Eyelets by Doodlebug, Tiny Gold Eyelets by Hyglo, Eyelet Setting Tool, Hammer by Simple Ideas, White Thread, Scissors, Black Micron Pen .02 by Sakura, Xyron Adhesive, Glue Pen by Zig

Tip: When using these teeny tiny eyelets, you may have to insert a pin to open up the hole after embossing to change their color. **Tip:** Use the Boy Hair bangs in front with the Girl Hair in back. You can also just trim the side view of Bitty Girl Hair or trim the bangs from the Bitty Ponytail Hair. **Tip:** To make the girl wave, just cut her arm off at the shoulder, and cut part of the Bitty Shorts from the waist to the crotch. Place shorts/sleeve over arm then secure to the page. **Tip:** I like the way that paper strips look on cards, but placing them through eyelets and tying them in knots can be a delicate operation. If paper strips are too much of a challenge, try using thin red ribbon instead. **Tip:** On the inside of the card where you usually write "Dear So and So", set a Small Cloud die on the spot. Chalk around it with blue chalk so that you have a light "outline" of the die. Now lift the die and shade where the perforation lines should be. Try this on background paper for cards and scrapbooking as well for a soft custom look.

Alternative Sayings:
"We'll miss you!"
"Have a Great Time!"

Actual Size: 8-5/8" wide x 4-3/4" high

HEART BORDER
CARD

SUPPLY LIST: Sizzix® Die Medium Border Heart **Paper** Little Sizzles™ Paper Pad "Pastels" and "Watercolors" by Sizzix™ **Miscellaneous** Magic Mesh, Scissors, Pink Writer Pen by Zig, Xyron Adhesive

Tip: Magic Mesh comes with an adhesive backing. Just place on your card and border with strips of white cardstock.

Alternate Use:
This is a super card to mass produce and even give to friends as gifts. No one ever has enough stationery!

Actual Size: 5-1/4" wide x 3-3/4" high

MESSAGE IN A BOTTLE
CARD

SUPPLY LIST: Sizzix® Dies Large Jar & Label, Large Scroll **Paper** Little Sizzles™ Paper Pad "Pastels" by Sizzix™ **Miscellaneous** Art Accentz™ "Terrifically Tacky Tape™" Sheets by Provo Craft®, Chalk by Craf-T Products, Cork by Craf-T Products, Twine, Tiny Seashells and Sea Stars, Sand (beach sand or craft sand work equally well), Scissors, Xyron Adhesive

Tip: This card is not for the faint of cardmaking heart! It would be a breeze if it wasn't for the "sealing up the sides" problem. There are two ways to make this card:
1. Seal the sides of the page protector well and pour in the sand. Hermafix dot adhesive works pretty well if you don't use too much sand. Seal all the edges (after putting in the rolled up Scroll). Realize that the recipient may very well get a little sandy when they open it! A little sand goes a long way on this one. Use that sand sparingly!
2. Cut a Terrifically Tacky Tape™ Sheet from 1/3 of the Jar. (This is where the sand would lay if the bottle was on its side.) Attach one side to the back of the bottle and cover the other side with sand. Attach the shells to this same side.

Tip: Cut the Jar on the fold along the side of the Jar, not the bottom. This way, you have to seal less of the area where the sand sits. **Tip:** Use the Label for the Jar to make the cork. Trim the sides just a little and you have the perfect cork stopper! **Tip:** Crinkle up the Scroll and chalk the edges and crinkles with brown chalk for a weathered look. You can also get the cardstock wet and crinkle for a super weathered look! **Tip:** A heat sealer does a better job of sealing the jar/bottle if you happen to have one, or you can sew the perimeter with a sewing machine.

Alternative Sayings:
"Bon Voyage"
"I Miss You"
"Hope to Hear From You Soon!"

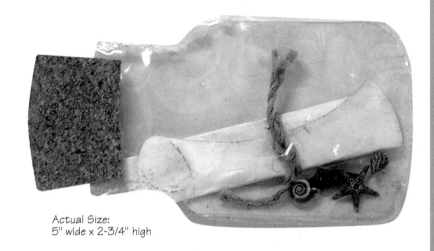

Actual Size:
5" wide x 2-3/4" high

BON VOYAGE
AIRPLANE CARD

SUPPLY LIST: Sizzix® Dies Large Stars, Medium Airplane, Small Megaphone **Paper** Color Wheel™ Cardstock Scrap Pad "Tropical" by Provo Craft®, Designer Paper "Zany Zoo Sky" by Provo Craft®, Black Cardstock **Miscellaneous** Alphabitties™ "Black Block Uppercase" by Provo Craft®, Black Beads by Darice, Black Embroidery Floss by DMC, Wire by Artistic Wire, Black Eyelets by Empress Rubber Stamps, Eyelet Setting Tool, Hammer by Simple Ideas, Scissors, Transfer Dots by Hermafix, Pop Dots

Tip: Send someone off on an exciting adventure with this colorful card. Spell out the destination with Alphabitties™ inside the flags. After they return from their trip, they can use this as a title on a scrapbook layout or on the cover of their vacation album! **Tip:** Trim and discard the handles from all of the Megaphones. These will be your "flags" that hang from your plane. Glue a single strand of floss on the inside of the flags, connecting the flags to each other and the Airplane, as shown.

Alternative Sayings:
"Bon Voyage"
"Farewell"
"Good-bye"
"Marry Me!"

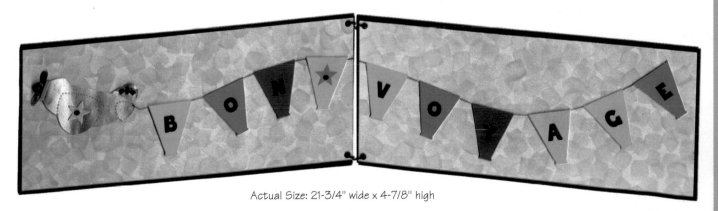

Actual Size: 21-3/4" wide x 4-7/8" high

Sizzix® Product List

Part #	Description	Part #	Description
38-0100	Large Die-Doll Body	38-0165	Large Die-Frame, Scallop
38-0101	Large Die-Doll Girl Hair #1	38-0166	Large Die-Frame, Jelly
38-0102	Large Die-Doll Boy Hair #1	38-0167	Medium Die-Banner
38-0103	Large Die-Doll Dresses	38-0168	Large Die-Wood Sign
38-0104	Large Die-Doll Overalls	38-0169	Large Die-Tent
38-0105	Medium Die-Doll Cowboy Access.	38-0170	Medium Die-Canoe & Paddle
38-0106	Large Die-Doll Winter Clothes	38-0171	Medium Die-Sand Or Snow Mound
38-0107	Medium Die-Doll Summer Clothes	38-0172	Medium Die-Fishing Pole
38-0108	Medium Die-Doll Summer Access.	38-0173	Small Die-Trout
38-0109	Medium Die-Doll Bath Clothes	38-0174	Small Die-Campfire
38-0110	Medium Die-Doll Bath Access.	38-0175	Small Die-Rocks
38-0111	Medium Die-Doll Bedtime Bear	38-0176	Large Die-Tree, Green
38-0112	Medium Die-Doll Bedtime Access.	38-0177	Large Die-Tree, Christmas
38-0113	Medium Die-Doll Graduation	38-0178	Large Die-Tree, Pine
38-0114	Small Die-Bitty Doll Body	38-0179	Medium Die Tree, Medium Pine
38-0115	Small Die-Bitty Girl Hair #1	38-0180	Medium Die-Cactus
38-0116	Small Die-Bitty Boy Hair #1	38-0181	Medium Die-Branch & Leaves
38-0117	Small Die-Bitty Shorts & Top	38-0182	Medium Die-Grass
38-0118	Small Die-Bitty Overalls	38-0183	Large Die-Tree, Palm
38-0119	Small Die-Bitty Swimsuit	38-0184	Large Die-Sun
38-0120	Small Die-Bitty Dresses	38-0185	Large Die-Cloud# 2
38-0121	Small Die-Bitty Pajamas & Bear	38-0186	Medium Die-Border, Mountain
38-0122	Small Die-Doll Sports Gear #1	38-0189	Small Die-Cloud #1
38-0123	Small Die-Doll Shoes #1	38-0190	Large Die-Basket, Picnic
38-0124	Large Die-Sailboat	38-0191	Large Die-Umbrella
38-0125	Medium Die-Car	38-0192	Medium Die-Splats
38-0126	Medium Die-Airplane	38-0193	Medium Die-Hot Dog
38-0127	Medium Die-Bicycle	38-0194	Medium Die-Ice Cream Cone
38-0128	Medium Die-Pool	38-0195	Medium Die-Ice Pop
38-0129	Medium Die-Bathtub	38-0196	Medium Die-Watermelon
38-0130	Medium Die Wave	38-0197	Small Die-Apple
38-0131	Medium Die-Road & Wavy Border	38-0198	Medium Die-Dolphin
38-0132	Large Die-Bus Back	38-0199	Medium Die-Sea Horse
38-0133	Large Die-Car Front	38-0200	Small Die-Fish
38-0134	Large Die-Motorcycle	38-0201	Small Die-Bubbles
38-0135	Large Die-Train Engine	38-0202	Small Die-Seashell # 1
38-0136	Large Die-Scooter	38-0203	Small Die-Seashell #2
38-0137	Medium Die-Wagon	38-0204	Small Die-Sand Dollar
38-0138	Large Die-Scroll	38-0205	Small Die-Starfish
38-0139	Large Die-Award	38-0207	Large Die-Tree, Bare
38-0140	Large Die-Filmstrip	38-0208	Large Die-Daisy #2
38-0141	Medium Die-Camera	38-0209	Medium Die-Flower, Rose
38-0142	Medium Die-Crayon	38-0210	Medium Die-Flower, Sunflower
38-0143	Medium Die-Pencil	38-0211	Medium Die-Flower, Tulip
38-0144	Small Die-Scissors	38-0212	Medium Die-Plant Pots
38-0145	Small Die-Photo Corners	38-0213	Medium Die-Fence, Picket
38-0146	Large Die-Balloons #2	38-0214	Medium Die-Leaves, Jungle
38-0147	Medium Die-Balloons #1	38-0215	Small Die-Leaf #1, Tiny
38-0148	Medium Die-Confetti	38-0216	Small Die-Leaf #2, Tiny
38-0149	Medium Die-Party Favor	38-0217	Small Die-Leaf #3, Tiny
38-0150	Medium Die-Party Hat	38-0218	Small Die-Leaf #1
38-0151	Medium Die-Candles	38-0219	Small Die-Leaf #2
38-0152	Medium Die-Gifts	38-0220	Small Die-Leaf #3
38-0153	Medium Die-Bow	38-0221	Small Die-Leaf #4
38-0154	Large Die-Stars	38-0222	Small Die-Leaf Trio
38-0155	Medium Die Stars, Primitive	38-0223	Small Die-Daisy Flower, Daisy #1
38-0156	Medium Die Border, Star	38-0224	Small Die Flower #1
38-0157	Large Die-Hearts	38-0226	Medium Die-Fern
38-0158	Medium Die-Hearts, Primitive	38-0227	Medium Die-Leaf, Stem
38-0159	Medium Die-Border, Heart	38-0228	Medium Die-Border, Ivy
38-0160	Medium Die-Swirls, Multi	38-0229	Medium Die-Butterfly #3
38-0161	Small Die- Swirl	38-0230	Small Die-Butterfly #1
38-0162	Large Die-Frame, Corner	38-0231	Small Die-Butterfly #2
38-0163	Large Die-Frame, Rectangle	38-0232	Small Die-Dragonfly
38-0164	Large Die-Frame, Zigzag	38-0233	Large Die-Santa Head